30
Rays of Hope

Rochie Rana

HEALTH HARMONY

an imprint of **B. JAIN PUBLISHERS (P) LTD.**
An ISO 9001 : 2000 Certified Company

30 Rays of Hope

Edition 2006

No part of this book may be reproduced, stored in a retrieval system or transmitted, in any form or by any means, mechanical, photocopying, recording or otherwise, without any prior written permission of the author.

© Copyright with the author

Price: Rs. 75.00

Published by **Kuldeep Jain** *for*

HEALTH HARMONY

an imprint of B. Jain Publishers (P) Ltd.
An ISO 9001 : 2000 Certified Company
1921, Street No. 10, Chuna Mandi,
Paharganj, New Delhi–110 055 (INDIA)
Phones: 91-11-2358 0800, 2358 1100, 2358 1300
Fax: 91-11-2358 0471; Email: bjain@vsnl.com
Website: www.bjainbooks.com

Printed in India by
J. J. Offset Printers
522, FIE, Patpar Ganj, Delhi–110 092
Phones: 91-11-2216 9633, 2215 6128

ISBN: 81-8056-672-2
BOOK CODE: BR-5901

Dedication

For the magic there is in living with the eyes of the soul wide open, and for those who taught me how to stay awake...

To my wonderful family and the people closest to my soul, who have all been my learning ground and pillars of strength and all those friends who have held me together in times of trial.

Especially for Daddy, my grandfather, who turns my life into a celebration!

Prologue

An invitation into the world of hope

Hope is the feeling that keeps us afloat in situations that threaten to engulf us and leave us with sadness and grief. It is also one of the three Christian virtues that help us go far in life, but in today's times when there are ever increasing reasons to feel demoralized, we need a handful of sunshine and a pocketful of promise to enable us to see the light at the end of the tunnel which is undoubtedly always there.

30 Rays of Hope is an endeavor to help people rediscover the assurance of hope and relive all the joy that life has to offer.

This book is meant to serve as a ready reckoner for the reader for all thirty days of the month. The book is an eclectic assortment of enlightening thoughts that are relevant to this era of stress and constant worry.

Introduction

Every chapter of this book contains words of encouragement in its first section. The subsequent section has a suggested exercise, meditation or tip that gives you an easy access to imbibe the goodness of a life in a simple to execute way. Every chapter closes with a prayer that is relevant to the theme of the chapter and can be chanted or read by to derive spiritual fulfillment from.

Each subject of every chapter has been carefully selected after two years of my counseling and I have thus chosen the thirty topics that are most commonly the reason for anxiety.

All the meditations and exercises have been developed in the last two years of my practice as a healer and have all been tried and studied before being suggested in the book.

The prayers mentioned in each chapter have been imbibed from various religions and cults from around the world and as such imbibe a sense of global spirit within them. The prayers are also an attempt to bring to light the fact that no matter what the religion and no matter what creed, all religions preach the same substance of humanity.

How to use the book

This book is meant to serve as a reckoner of your daily measure of inner peace and tranquility.

The book consists of 30 chapters, one for each day of the month and each chapter contains one section of reflections, one of meditational exercises and the last section that consists of prayers from around the world. While the reflections will start you on a journey of introspection of the self, the meditational tips will enable you to imbibe the goodness of inner harmony in practical ways and there is no better way to start a day than with a prayer.

Use this book as a guide that will enable you, every day of the month, to enhance your life and to bring out the best in you!

Inside

Dedication	iii
Prologue	iv
Indroduction	v
How to use the book	vi
1 Beauty of the Cosmos	2
2 The Miracles of the Infinitesimal	09
3 Kindness is Your Greatest Tool	14
4 What you Choose is what Makes you !	19
5 The Thing of Beauty is a Joy Forever	25
6 Celebrate Tears	30
7 Relationships Always Lie Beyond Boundaries	36
8 Live Dangerously	43
9 Bring your Ego to Ground Zero	49
10 This too Shall Pass ...	54
11 An Apology is the Superglue of Life	60
12 Love Conquers All	66
13 Nurture your Experiences, they are the Source of all Wisdom	72
14 Forgiveness is the Key to Mend What Lies Broken	77
15 The Blank Paper Syndrome	83
16 Float upon the Stream, Embrace Everyone on the Way	88

17	Be Patient Towards all that is Unanswered Within	94
18	Stay Awake	100
19	Truth Comes in Shades of Gray	106
20	Seek Beonyd the Self	111
21	Once Connected Two Souls Can Never Part	118
22	The Ready Reckoner to Live	124
23	Walk Beyond Time	130
24	Raise the Dust of Change on the Road to Life	136
25	Everyone is a Healer	141
26	The Right Recipe for the Perfect Speech	147
27	Make Big Plans and Deliver !!	152
28	Hearing the Sounds of Silence	158
29	Dream Big and Aim for the Moon	164
30	Celebrate Life as if it Were Your Last Day	170

Epilogue   180

Peace Invocation

Om taccham yoravrini mahe
Ghatun yajnaya
Ghatun yajnapataye
Daivi svastirastu naha
Svastir manushebhyaha
Urdhvam jigatu bheshajam
Sham no astu dvipade
Sham chatushpade

OM SHANTIH SHANTIH SHANTIH

We worship and pray to the Supreme Lord for the welfare of all beings.

May all miseries and shortcomings leave us forever so that we may always sing for the Lord during the holy fire ceremonies.

May all medicinal herbs grow in potency so that all diseases may be cured.

May the gods rain peace on us.

May all the two-legged creatures be happy, and may all the four-legged creatures also be happy.

May there be peace in the hearts of all beings in all realms.

THE PURUSHA SUKT

1.
Beauty of the Cosmos

Nature is our biggest teacher. We are but a diminutive manifestation of the greater cosmos. Nature changes always but this change is the constant itself. Nature flows from season to season, as does the heart. The heart too, sees eternal spring as it suffers many unending autumns and it is in times like such that we should draw our inspiration from nature. Jonas Salk once said, "Life is magic, the way nature works seems to be quite magical."

The barren trees of autumn do not look frail in their deprivation; instead they stand erect in their certainty of the spring to come. Similarly for the soul that feels weary, exhausted and defeated, there is always the promise of a beautiful spring at the end of a merciless autumn. Life is such that it will encompass happiness and pain both, but the greatness of human nature lies in embracing both as seasons of the heart and living out every moment of the joy and the pain.

When we are feeling a state of immense joy and fulfillment, we feel a sense of contentment with life at large and the world feels beautiful. It is in times like these that the heart believes in the glory of God and the Godliness of love but when the heart slips into sadness for life is a balance of both, then our belief in people around us and ourselves seems to dither. We begin to question everything; from who we are to if our reasons for happiness were ever real and true? That is when our memory erases all history of moments spent at peace with our loved ones and ourselves.

Have you looked around you, at market places and grocery stores that every season has a special fruit to it? While ripe and juicy oranges are best available in winter, the most succulent apples are fruits of spring. So it is nature trying to tell us that there is a season for everything, and as much as one would favor the warmth of a spring afternoon, winter too comes with its sunlit days. Similarly for our lives, we might always want to remain happy, with spring in our steps but when in agony, our heart is trying to chisel our souls to understand human emotions better and to know for ourselves the difference between a smile and tears.

Seasons of the heart are like the spells of time; they will never remain the same, for if nature's splendor is ever changing then so shall the seasons of the heart. We should not simply make peace with the fact that there will be moments of agony and grief in our lives but we must on the contrary; learn to celebrate even the moments of misery and loneliness in our lives, it only through our celebration that we will learn to live our lives to the fullest.

Winter spells and summer days
Are never at mercy of nature's ways
When life is bliss, it's a chirrupy spring
When the heart is in pain, its what the
  winter brings.

Tip

If you truly wish to take pleasure in nature, then take out a day when you are supposed to meet your friends at a customary pub or a coffee house and instead of these standard places, get together at a park or a friend's farmhouse, even your own garden will do.

Give others and your own self an opportunity to appreciate nature and it will be an effort that will reap rich rewards.

Prayer

Father of Light! Great God of Heaven!
Hear'st thou the accents of despair?
Can guilt like man's be ever forgiven?
Can vice atone for crimes by prayer?

Father of Light, on thee I call!
Thou seest my soul is dark within;
Thou who canst mark the sparrow's fall,
Avert from me the death of sin.

No shrine I seek, to sects unknown;
Oh, point to me the path of truth!
Thy dread omnipotence I own;
Spare, yet amend, the faults of youth.

Let bigots rear a gloomy fane,
Let superstition hail the pile,
Let priests, to spread their sable reign,
With tales of mystic rites beguile.

Shall man confine his Maker's sway
To Gothic domes of moldering stone?

Thy temple is the face of day;
Earth, ocean, heaven, thy boundless throne.
Shall man condemn his race to hell,
Unless they bend in pompous form?
Tell us that all, for one who fell,
Must perish in the mingling storm?

Shall each pretend to reach the skies,
Yet doom his brother to expire,
Whose soul a different hope supplies,
Or doctrines less severe inspire?

Shall these by creeds they can't expound,
Prepare a fancied bliss or woe?
Shall reptiles, groveling on the ground
Their great Creator's purpose know?

Shall those, who live for self-alone,
Whose years float on in daily crime
Shall they by Faith for guilt atone,
And live beyond the bounds of Time?

Father! No prophet's laws I seek,
Thy laws in Nature's works appear;
I own myself corrupt and weak,
Yet will I pray, for thou wilt hear!

Thou, who canst guide the wandering star,
Through trackless realms of æther's space;

Who calm'st the elemental war,
Whose hand from pole to pole I trace:
Thou, who in wisdom placed me here,
Who, when thou wilt, canst take me hence,
Ah! Whilst I tread this earthly sphere,
Extend to me thy wide defense.

To Thee, my God, to thee I call!
Whatever weal or woe betide,
By thy command I rise or fall.
In thy protection I confide.

If, when this dust to dust's restored,
My soul shall float on airy wing,
How shall thy glorious name adored
Inspire her feeble voice to sing!

But if this fleeting spirit share
With clay the grave's eternal bed,
While life yet throbs I raise my prayer,
Though doom'd no more to quit the dead.

THE PRAYER OF NATURE
Lord Byron

2.
The Miracles of the Infinitesimal

It has been said many a times but it is truly astounding that all the greatness of nature lies in the smallest of its wonders. Have you ever taken the time out to sit down by a lake and observe, as the sun seems to melt into the coolness of the waters of the lake? To watch the intensity of a glistening sun plunge into its horizon changing its hues into resplendent purples and pinks is the most awe-inspiring moment that life could offer.

It is nature symbolizing human life to perfection. As St. Bernard of Clairvaux quoted, "Believe one who knows you will find something more in woods than in books. Trees and stones will teach you that which you can never learn from masters." If something as majestic as the life giving sun must fade away for a black sooty night of darkness then how can our mortal lives remain unaffected by grief and sadness? But just as the sun loses its brilliance only to rise stronger in all its glory, the darkness of our lives is also only momentary after which there is the promise of certain light that will alleviate all the moments of agony in one fleeting moment of blithe joy.

We often tend to understand the night for all its darkness and the heavy feeling of brooding that it brings with it but the night also holds within itself, the truth about light. If it were not for the darkness, how else could we know the difference between shadows and light? How else would we know the meaning of that one breath that separates sadness and elation? In tune with the same, David Nicholas had once said that "God's promises are like the stars, the darker the night, the brighter they shine."

Taking a leaf from the page of nature and the interplay of night and day, we understand that as much as the heart may hurt and as much as there might be a defeated spirit within us, all we need to do is keep our head held high and believe in the light at the end of the tunnel because energy follows thoughts and if we believe that at the end of the journey of sorrow, there will be innate lightness then the world will conspire to bring that happiness to our doorstep.

"One may not reach the dawn save by the path of the night"
Kahlil Gibran

Reflection

This is a meditation that can be done at dusk or a bit later in the evening. Take out some time from your schedule of the day and walk up to your window, garden or the balcony, the objective is to be able to see outside and observe the sky.

As you walk towards the balcony, take small but meaningful steps, with each step leaving behind all your worries and anxiety of the day. As you reach the garden or your windowpane, look upwards at the sky and observe the birds in the sky, this is the time that all the birds finish whatever they had to do in the day, look for food, feed their young ones, make a nest etc and they flock together for an inviting night of rest.

As you observe the birds, try and internalize the same, no matter how hard your day has been or how aggrieved you are with a certain problems, be like the birds, come dusk and you will push all your worries aside for the day and let your soul breathe, free of worries and tension, at least for the course of the night.

Once you begin to make a habit of the same, it will start coming very naturally to you to deal with your problems afresh and with a mind and soul that has got adequate rest over the evening and you will begin to live anew and this will be your lesson learnt from nature.

Prayer

To Thee I breathe my humble strain,
Grateful for all thy mercies past,
And hope, my God, to thee again
This erring life may fly at last.
May the angels keep you till morning.
May they guide you through the night.
May they comfort all your sorrows.
May they help you win the fight.
May they keep watch on your soul.
May they show you better ways.
May they guard you while you're sleeping.
May they see you through your days.
May they show you new hopes.
May they still your every doubt.
May they calm your every fear.
May they hear you when you shout.
May the angels keep you till morning.
More than this I cannot pray.
And if the angels ever fail you.
Then may God be there that day.

ANONYMOUS

3.
Kindness is Your Greatest Tool

Let the kindness within you brim over into limitless hearts and its countries.

A human being is what God made us but being human is something that we will have to learn, as we grow older. Compassion is but one word that holds in it the many secrets of kindness that grows treble merely by sharing. As William Penn said, "I expect to pass through life but once. If therefore, there be any kindness I can show, or any good thing that I can do to any fellow being, let me do it now, for I shall not pass through this way again." A twenty four hour day feels insufficient for many and with so much to pack in so little time one would naturally wonder where to source the time from, to do a good deed or to show compassion to someone, but in reality one need not make time to be kind, just simply continue being kind in whatever that you do and whoever that you meet. Lao Tzu once said, "Kindness in words creates confidence. Kindness in thinking creates profoundness. Kindness in giving creates love."

Sometimes kindness lies in being a good listening post to another person and sometimes it lies in encircling the arms and giving someone a life saving hug. Compassion is simply the act of passing on the good moments of life to another person when they need it the most. Like Wordsworth had aptly said, "that best portion of a good man's life - his little, nameless, unremembered acts, of kindness and of love." You might forget after doing a good deed or being kind to someone but to the person whom the act of kindness is directed, will never forget you or to mention you in his / her prayers. As also Neil Strait extended the thought, "Kindness is more than deeds. It is an attitude, an expression, a look, a touch. It is anything that lifts another person."

One does not have to go out finding the spirit of goodness, it lies within everyone's hearts albeit in deeper countries of it and we need to look inwards with faith and purity and there we will find the benevolence of faith and integrity hidden under the layer of worldly wisdom and sedition and once we access the source of our goodness then it will always flow like a boundless river and touch everyone's hearts wherever we go. As Mother Teresa said "Let no one ever come to you without leaving better and happier. Be the living expression of God's kindness: kindness in your face, kindness in your eyes, kindness in your smile."

Tip

Make a journal for yourself, an extraordinary journal, and call it the kindness journal. Every day as you retire to bed, write down at least five acts of kindness that you have carried out in your day and after seven consecutive days of having repeated the same act of kindness, negate that from your list since chances are that the oft repeated act would have become a part of your life by then.

Aim to add more and more acts of kindness to your journal everyday till you reach a point where you feel satiated at the number and value of good deeds that you have performed in the day.

Prayer

Oh, that You would bless me indeed,
And enlarge my territory,
That Your hand would be with me,
And that You would keep me from evil,
That I may not cause pain!

The prayer of jabez - 1 chronicles 4:10 (nkjv)

4.

What you choose is What Makes You!

We often tend to sit back and feel misery for ourselves, a sort of self-sympathy where we feel helpless at the hands of life. In my practice as a healer, it is very often that I have come across people feeling sorry for themselves, blaming others for what is happening in their lives and feeling helplessness with the situation. Gerald D Bell says, "You are 100% responsible for your own happiness. Other people are not responsible. Your parents aren't responsible. Your spouse isn't. You alone are. So, if you are not happy, it's up to you to change something. It is not up to someone else to 'fix it' for you."

When we came into this world, we were born with all the qualities that it takes for us to be successful human beings and as time passes in an individual's life, our ability to understand, comprehend and emote become more enhanced. At every stage of life, it gives us choices. The choice to behave in a certain way, the choice to learn a certain lesson, the choice to feel in a particular way and although most often we do not perceive ourselves as making these choices, it is in fact we ourselves who decide to do a particular thing in a particular way and thus its corresponding consequences.

Take for instance eating porridge for breakfast; it is a subliminal choice because we might not have the time for a full-fledged meal in the mornings. If the porridge assists us in losing weight or maintaining it, then it is a mere consequence of a simple choice that we had made maybe even without giving it too much thought.

The same principle applies to the larger and more intense things in life. When we decide to be with someone because they pull at the strings of the heart and if at some phases of the relationship we do face some pain and hurt, it is a consequence of the choice of being in the relationship that we had made and thus we cannot entirely thrust the blame of our sorrow on to another person no matter how easy and convenient that might be.

If we lose someone or something close to our hearts, we can choose to feel sorry for ourselves and lose ourselves in a vortex of melancholy or we could choose to celebrate the existence of that person or thing in our lives till as long as they were a part of it and making that choice will be the parameter of whether we will be lost in self pity for a long time to come or rejoicing everything that life brings to us. As Thich Nhat Hanh said, "Sometimes your joy is the source of your smile, but sometimes your smile can be the source of your joy."

Exercise

Take some time out for yourself in the day, a time when you are with yourself alone, when nobody will disturb you. Take this time out to rethink your pain and angst. Take a piece of paper and a pen and write down the reason for your distress and then make a small chart about what incidents led to the situation. As you make the chart, it will come to light, the circumstances where you made certain decisions that have led you to where you are right now.

Making a chart will help you understand with clarity that you are not a mere victim in your suffering and that you too have played a role in making your choices. Once you comprehend what went wrong where after listing all situations clearly, then you will be able to come out of your grief and agony sooner.

Sometimes the written word explains things better than thoughts that are wordless in the mind since such thoughts are prone to taking on abstract meanings as well, but the minute that you put things on paper, life at large and the worries at hand will appear to you in a new and objective perspective and not only will that enable you to understand the problem better, it will also help you address the problem in a better way.

Prayer

Almighty and Eternal God,
Give me, I beseech You,
The great gift of inward peace.
Command the winds and storms,
Of my unruly passions.
Subdue, by Your grace,
My proneness to love,
Created things too much.
Give me a love of suffering for Your sake.
Make me forbearing and kind to others,
That I may avoid quarrels and contentions.
And teach me constantly to seek after
And to acquire that perfect resignation
To Your Holy Will
Which alone brings interior peace.
Amen.

CATHOLIC PRAYER

5.
A Thing of Beauty is a Joy Forever

"A thing of beauty is a joy forever" is the everlasting first line of the poem 'Endymion' by John Keats and it still holds true years after they were first penned. Beauty, many say is a subjective outlook and that according to the world famous Aesop's fables; beauty lies in the eyes of the beholder, but one thing is for certain, that beauty lies all around us at all times, all we need to do is take a closer look at the vast treasures of immaculate beauty and our heart will never cease to experience wonderment. And even for the cynics, there is hope in the words of John Constable who said "I never saw an ugly thing in my life: for let the form of an object be what it may—light, shade, and perspective will always make it beautiful."

We often feel that beauty is a limit concept, only meant to be seen and appreciated on a woman's face or an awe-inspiring work of art and sometimes in the display of nature but the truth is that beauty is in everything that surrounds us.

Beauty lies in a moment lived with a loved one, it lies in the embrace of a mother and child, it lies in getting drenched in the rain together, it is on the face of a puppy when it is happy to see you, on the face of an underprivileged child when you take out the time to feed him / her. John Cage in his life gave out some pearls of wisdom when he said, "The first question I ask myself when something doesn't seem to be beautiful is why do I think it's not beautiful. And very shortly you discover that there is no reason."

If we decide to look at the world through the eyes of a child, then we will begin to understand and appreciate beauty in an enhanced way. A child has an intrinsic ability to make beautiful, even the greatest of chaos. I have often observed that when we give a child simple playing blocks, they will arrange them in a very aesthetically appealing pattern that will resemble a paragon of beauty. Such is the intense understanding that a child has, of both beauty and adventure.

Our notion of beauty is limited only to our perception, the day we open our eyes and our hearts to the marvels of nature around us, even the smallest gesture and the most mundane sunset will seem remarkable to us and once the eyes of the heart are taught to appreciate the many facets of beauty then much like learning how to ride a bicycle, we will never unlearn the art of perceiving beauty in its many forms. As John Greenleaf Whittier said, "Beauty once seen is never lost."

Tip

Make one area of your home, the sanctified corner of beauty. In this space, put all the objects that inspire you and remind you of how exquisite things and people are in your life. Fill this corner with fresh flowers, things that you have created with your own hands and photographs of people whom you love.

Let this corner be your constant reminder of the splendor around you and ensure that you pass through this corner often in your day. Unadulterated moments of elation are a guarantee each time you pass by this corner.

Prayer

Almighty God, the Great
Thumb we cannot evade to
Tie any knot;
The Roaring Thunder that splits mighty trees:
The all-seeing Lord up on high who sees
Even the footprints of an antelope on
A rock mass here on Earth.
You are the one who does
Not hesitate to respond to our call.
You are the cornerstone of peace.

NATIVE AMERICAN PRAYER

6.
Celebrate Tears

Tears are a gift, not only to our eyes but a gift meant for our hearts as well. Very often, in my practice as a healer I have come across people who may be facing the worst of all calamities but have rendered themselves incapable of crying. They feel that crying is an act of weakness and if they let tears flow down their cheeks then it will be a sign of their incapability of dealing with the situation at hand.

On the contrary, tears are a healing potion; they are a means by which the heart and mind will cure themselves of their grief. Alfred Austin says of tears, "Tears are the summer showers to the soul." When a teardrop falls from the eye on to the cheek, its warmth is a sign of reassurance; it is an indication of the body healing itself. Denying ourselves the opportunity to express our distress by crying whole-heartedly means putting off our chances of healing faster. Oliver Wendell Holmes says, "Laughter and tears are meant to turn the wheels of the same machinery of sensibility; one is wind-power, and the other water-power; that is all."

Tears are a celebration as well if we choose to perceive them as that, they are also God's gift to us as much as smiles and mirth are, we only must look at crying as something that also brings us positivity by ridding the body of pent up negative emotions. Holding on to sadness does not cure us of it; instead it creates repressive emotions that will only scar our minds and souls for all out lives. Nicholas Cage, the famous actor echoes these thoughts when he quotes that "I cry a lot. My emotions are very close to my surface. I don't want to hold anything in so it festers and turns into pus - a pustule of emotion that explodes into a festering cesspool of depression."

Tears are a lot like rain, when the earth is hot and in pain, the clouds burst forth bringing with them, the potion that will put the earth at peace. Similar to the rain are our tears as well, when the heart is grieved and at the edge of all reason, it is only then that tears burst forth, bringing with them, a cure for the ailing heart.

The Holy Guru Granth Sahib says, "Tera bhana meetha lage" which in translation means "anything that God gifts us is sweet to our souls and we accept it as such", this is an indication that if God has brought us to a period in life where we have to embrace tears then we shall do so humbly and consider them the fruits of love from God Himself. Also, Victor Hugo believes that "If suffer we must, let's suffer on the heights."

If we learn to accept our tears as we accept our moments of joy, which is when we will truly learn to live our lives to the optimum. Thomas Merton once said, "The truth that many people never understand, until it is too late, is that the more you try to avoid suffering the more you suffer because smaller and more insignificant things begin to torture you in proportion to your fear of being hurt." So, make an effort to accept your suffering and appreciate the tears in your eyes as signs of being alive, truly alive!

Exercise

Whenever you are feeling pain and misery, let yourself go, hand yourself over to your tears, they alone heal the soul and to repress our tears would mean closing the doors of our hearts to our inner physician. Be with yourself and cry out all the sadness and grief within you, let your face feel warm with the feeling of tears staining it. Cry till you cannot cry anymore.

Then proceed to make yourself a warm cup of milk and pull out the one book or film that always inevitably tends to make you feel good on the inside, then make yourself snug and warm and indulge whole heartedly in watching the film or reading the book. While on the binge, order yourself your favorite dessert since crying tends to make the sugar levels in the body dip a bit, allowing yourself a sweet treat will lift your spirits and make you feel better by leaps and bounds.

Follow this with the third step of calling a friend who knows you inside out and is your best listening post. Empty your heart out to the friend and see how much better you will feel. Alternatively, if you do not want to share your tears with someone, take up a pen and paper and jot down all that you are feeling, write till as long as your words do not get exhausted and read what you have written. Often this will not only give you a perspective on the problem, it also is a great way of letting out your sadness and not hold on to it for longer than is needed.

Prayer

Dear Lord,
I have shed tears from my eyes today
In pain and in grief
My life feels as though it has thickened in my veins
And in my moment of pain Dear Lord,
Give me the strength to see through the tears
Give me the strength to hear what my tears are trying to tell me
Allow me to celebrate these tears
For you have thought my eyes worthy of them
And everything that you bless me with
Is higher to me than the greatest truth.

Prayer to celebrate tears

7.

*R*elationships *A*lways *L*ie *B*eyond *B*oundaries

Sometimes we meet some people in our lives who connect to our hearts instantly, in moments when we do not feel the strain of caste, creed, age or gender. In but one moment everything that we have known in our lives becomes inconsequential, fading away into nothingness, leaving behind only an abstract feeling of unity with that one person, of having known that person forever, even beyond time, and you could have met that person for the first time only five minutes ago. As Flavia Weedn said, "Some people come into our lives and leave footprints on our hearts and we are never ever the same."

Such is the power of Karmic connections, something that the mind might take long to understand but the heart accepts instantaneously. It is in such situations that we try hard to name the emotions that the person evokes within us because we as human beings have been conditioned to name every emotion, put a tag on them and place them neatly on the shelves of our minds. The truth is that some relationships need no name and to try and put them in a designated position in our structured lives is futile.

For some relationships, naming them means tying them within boundaries that they do not deserve. Such relationships should only be lived out with each passing moment and not be coerced into shapes and contours, which would only turn such God blessed relationships into mere silhouettes of what they would be if liberated from the periphery of figure and form.

We often start getting caught up in the web of social obligations and feel indebted to give every relationship a name, classify it and live it thus but in reality, names are what we humans have created because we have the gift of language and relationships that are formed as a result of a cosmic union are not at the mercy of names or explanation and should be lived out as such. Sometimes excessive definition of a thing or a relationship can bereave it of its spirit, its very essence and thus, some relationships should be felt not explained. Antoine de Saint-Exupéry says of relationships, "Man is a knot into which relationships are tied."

All relationships and essentially the ones that feel tied to the heart and soul should be seen from the eyes of a dream. As Hugh Elliot says, "Just because you love someone doesn't mean you have to be involved with them. Love is not a bandage to cover wounds". Nothing lasts forever but the moments lived in loving someone honestly from the innermost depths of the heart should be felt in the heart and traced within the soul forever and subsequently even if we were to part with the other person, we would feel no sense of loss because the person would have become a living breathing part of us, never to be separated from us, even in death.

Tip

In case you have parted ways with someone you love, pull out their picture and cry your heart out, mourning is the finest way of dealing with separation. If you don't allow your grief to heal you, chances are you might never be ready to love again but remember that this melancholy too shall pass and when you want to distract yourself, call a friend who understands you and your grief, go out with this friend for a stroll or a film and that should take care of you for a while.

Remember always that it's all right to feel pain and if your grief gets too much for you to handle, pull out a band-aid and stick it on your heart, which should make your heart feel protected.

Prayer

*From the sweet-scented streams of
Thine eternity give me to drink,*

*O my God, and of the fruits of the tree of
Thy being enable me to taste,*

*O my Hope! From the crystal springs of
Thy love suffer me to quaff,*

O my Glory, and beneath the shadow of Thine everlasting providence let me abide,

*O my Light! Within the meadows of Thy nearness, before
Thy presence, make me able to roam,*

*O my Beloved, and at the right hand of the throne of Thy
mercy, seat me,*

*O my Desire! From the fragrant breezes of Thy joy let a
breath pass over me,*

O my Goal, and into the heights of the paradise of Thy

reality let me gain admission,
O my Adored One! To the melodies of the dove of Thy oneness suffer me to hearken,

O Resplendent One, and through the spirit of Thy power and Thy might quicken me,

O my Provider! In the spirit of Thy love keep me steadfast, O my Succorer, and in the path of Thy good pleasure set firm my steps,

O my Maker! Within the garden of Thine immortality, before Thy countenance, let me abide forever,

O Thou who art merciful unto me, and upon the seat of Thy glory establish me,

O Thou Who art my Possessor! To the heaven of Thy loving-kindness lift me up,

O my Quickener, and unto the Daystar of Thy guidance lead me,

O Thou my Attractor! Before the revelations of Thine invisible spirit summon me to be present,

O Thou Who art my Origin and my Highest Wish, and unto the essence of the fragrance of Thy beauty, which Thou wilt manifest, cause me to return,

O Thou Who art my God! Potent art Thou to do what pleaseth Thee. Thou art, verily, the Most Exalted, the All Glorious, and the All Highest.

BAHÁ'U'LLÁH

8.

Live Dangerously

In today's day and age when we all have set innumerable goals for ourselves, we tend to feel exhausted and tired, not just physically but emotionally as well. At the end of every day, we feel a sense of fatigue and all we want to do every day of our lives is take a break from work but we do not allow ourselves the liberty of taking a break because that would mean a hurdle or time delay in achieving our goals.

Our desires to achieve tangible things become our set life goals and the restlessness to get to the targets makes us feel incapable as well leading our self esteem to suffer and for life to slowly begin falling apart. Learn to let go every now and then, live a little dangerously, as James B. Conant said, "Behold the turtle. He makes progress only when he sticks his neck out."

The truth lies in abandoning a report card oriented life where we mark ourselves everyday in how much closer we are to attaining our desires. We should discard the want to conquer anything in life and learn to live with abandon and liveliness that comes naturally to all animals and humans alike. When we allow ourselves to be freed from controlled expectations that we line up for ourselves, that is when the openness of our nature comes to the fore and we reach a sense of illumination where everything becomes fluid in our lives, nothing remains coerced and attempted, it all becomes a sense of flowing with the rivers of the world, moving from once sentiment of realization and accomplishment to another without having to restrain ourselves or our responses. Johann Wolfgang von Goethe said about this, "Live dangerously and you live right!"

Look around you and you will find that all trees, rivers, mountains and hills are standing with gay abandon, willing to embrace all the seasons that come to them, they are at the mercy of nobody and have not a thing to prove to anybody, they exist to blend in with nature, live as such and then melt back into the elements of the universe. If we try and emulate the same, even if every now and then, we will feel better connected to nature and also tap within our souls, a spirit that connects us to the greater cosmos. As Friedrich Nietzsche puts it, "The secret of reaping the greatest fruitfulness and the greatest enjoyment from life is to live dangerously!"

Living like the wind and water that make us is not easily achievable because we are taught since childhood to control our responses, constantly push ourselves to set and achieve goals but if we set our minds to it and slowly imbibe life like a river flowing within us, then that would take us to the threshold of spiritual enlightenment.

Exercise

Pick a day, which is light for you as far as appointments for the day or pending work is concerned, it could be a weekend or another day of the week depending on your work schedule.

After having picked a day, think of the one thing that you would love to do but are scared to do it or simply do not have the time to indulge in. this could be anything from watching a play or going Para-gliding. Pick the one activity closest to your heart that you have truly been longing to do and schedule this activity on the day when you are relatively free.

If you desire, then take a friend along, someone who will appreciate the activity, which you have chosen to undertake and maybe even participate as enthusiastically. If you cannot find someone who shares the passion with you, never mind; do not allow that to be a reason for not going through with what you have chosen.

Go ahead and indulge yourself, give yourself the well deserved prize of living life for once the way you want to lead it, throwing caution to the winds can be a good thing every now and then. After you have gone ahead and done what it takes to please yourself, see what a difference it makes to your subsequent days. Your soul, mind and body will feel awakened and rejuvenated and it will make you a more affable person than before as well.

Once you get into the groove of it, make it a habit to indulge yourself once every while. Set your own limits for cautious living and live dangerously occasionally, it's the only way of achieving perfect balance!

Prayer

*I will not die an unlived life. I will not live in fear of
falling or catching fire. I choose to
Inhabit my days, to allow my living to open me, to make
me less afraid, more accessible, to loosen my
Heart until it becomes a wing, a torch, and a promise. I
choose to risk my significance; to live so that
Which came to me as seed goes to the next as blossom
and that which came to me as blossom, goes on as fruit.*

FULLY ALIVE - DAWNA MARKOVA

9.
Bring Your Ego to Ground Zero

I spent my growing years in a missionary school and had moral science class every day. The most important lesson that I remember having learnt was 'do unto others as you would like them to do unto you'. That was a mere sentence but it carried the weight of all worldly knowledge in it. We as human beings are conferred with the responsibility to primarily love all others simply because we have been granted the ability to do so.

What happens very often as we are growing up is that the self starts becoming more important to us than everyone else around us. We begin to think for ourselves first, which is not incorrect but in doing so we forget to consider our responsibilities towards other people. As Samuel Butler had once said, "The truest characters of ignorance are vanity, and pride and arrogance."

It is our duty to never hurt anybody intentionally and to never step on anyone's toes to get to our destination because as the very famous proverb goes 'what goes around, comes around', and that holds true for everyone universally. The self becomes the center of our universe, we become our own axis, 'I' becomes the be all and end all of our existence and we begin to perceive things from one concentrated point of view; ourselves. George Sand had once said, "Vanity is the quicksand of reason" and it is indeed true for when we become self important in our own opinion, then we fail to see any reason and that is when the downward journey of our life is heralded.

When we start pursuing goals and targets for ourselves alone, that is when we begin to disregard other people entirely and we may seem flippant to all those around us who truly matter to us. The obsession with the self is the root cause of us grieving other people since we put ourselves first; we fail to consider another's feelings and emotions. The more we disregard others in the pursuit of our own glory, the more we will find ourselves disconnected with everything around us, as Thomas Wolfe rightly said, "The surest cure for vanity is loneliness."

If we have pained or caused grief to someone with our actions, knowing that we are doing so, we might feel that we will get away with it, after all nature has bigger issues to deal with than what one person has done unto another, but we forget that nature balances everything, from the smallest amoeba to the supreme universe in its equivocal character of justice.

Eventually, if we have cheated someone or caused him or her grief then we too shall suffer the same agony, perhaps not at the hands of the very person whom we have hurt but at the hands of someone else who would be nature's tool of rendering justice. One fact that remains eternally true is that nobody can escape the code of justice and thus if we decide to never be the reason of someone's tears then by a passive action we are ensuring that our Karma does not get tainted with the immensity of an immoral deed.

Tip

When you think you have hurt someone, immediately say sorry but do so only if you feel it from the bottom of your heart, re-think what you have done or said to the other person to offend them. Ensure that you apologize face to face and if that is not possible then do so over the phone and remember that the other person is probably hurt over the issue and so they may behave unreasonably but you must take that in your stride.

After you are done apologizing, follow it up with flowers or a letter that reiterates your apology and that is indisputably going to heal anything gone wrong in a relationship.

Prayer

I confess to almighty God, and to you, my brothers and sisters, that I have sinned through my own fault, in my thoughts and in my words, in what I have done and what I have failed to do;
And I ask blessed Mary, ever virgin, all the angels and saints, and you, my brothers and sisters, to pray for me to the Lord our God.

A CATHOLIC PRAYER

10.
This too Shall Pass...

Life sometimes brings us to a stage where we feel as if we are being put to some kind of test. Everything around us seems to be going off beam, there is a distressing feeling of not being understood and it feels as if everyone around us has turned their backs on us and that we would give anything to feel some assuring words of comfort.

It is in such chapters of life that we should re-think the testing times and understand with depth and emotion that the times of stress are a way of nature chaffing our soul and giving it the strength to deal with greater problems if they were to ever arise. Benjamin Disraeli was of the opinion that "Despair is the conclusion of fools" and it holds true in all aspects, only a weak hearted person would allow despair to be his / her undoing because a fighter would make the same despair his strength, like Edmund Burke had once said, "Never despair; but if you do, work on in despair."

Diamonds that glisten their way into our hearts and become a woman's best friends are the leading example of nature to show us the way through such moments of test. A diamond is coal to begin with; dark and unfinished in the womb of nature and it is this very Mother Nature that puts it through immense pressure and strain, only then does the meager coal turn into the much coveted diamond. As Kahlil Gibran says, " is not the cup that holds your wine the very cup that was burned in the potter's oven?"

Life too, will test only the strongest of shoulders, it is the law of nature, the stronger the spirit, the more it is put to test. Nature leaves the greatest trials to those whom it deems capable enough to pass them with flying colors. If in such moments of being put to test, our spirit weakens and we concede defeat, we have truly lost all reason to live, for obstacles are but the pebbles that make up the rocky terrain of life, but to lose our spirit to such challenges means letting our optimism and hope run out through our fingers and that is when we would have truly lost our all.

Life does what it must, constantly hurl obstructions our way and we should do what life expects of us in such situations, fight the hindrances with valor and gallantry for lucky are those whose sanguinity and fortitude is tested at the altar of the greatest teacher of all, time itself.

"God does not send us despair in order to kill us; he sends it in order to awaken us to new life."

HERMANN HESSE

Exercise

Whenever you are feeling high strung in life, pressurized and worried, and are faced with intense stress, then the best thing to do is to walk up to a puppy or any other small animal; the pet could be your own or you could reach out to a friend or relative to borrow one for a few hours.

Caressing animals and playing with them has been scientifically approved as being therapeutic and there is no better natural remedy than that to bust stress. Seat yourself on the floor to be able to face the puppy or kitten directly and then watch them as they jump all over you and tug you to play with them. Caress them and they will always reciprocate with a lick of their tongue on your hand or a howl or joy.

When you get down to playing with a pet, see how difficult it becomes for you to remain anxious or feel pressurized, and once you can shirk the feeling of pressure from your mind, that's the time when you should resume thinking about what is causing you the stress without being threatened to cave under it.

Prayer

Thou Whose tests are a healing medicine to such as are nigh unto Thee,

Whose sword is the ardent desire of all them that love Thee,

Whose dart is the dearest wish of those hearts that yearn after Thee,

Whose decree is the sole hope of them that have reconized Thy truth!

I implore Thee, by Thy divine sweetness and by the splendors of the glory of Thy face,

To send down upon us from Thy retreats on high that which will enable us to draw nigh unto Thee.

Set, then, our feet firm, O my God, in Thy Cause, and enlighten our hearts with the effulgence of Thy knowledge, and illumine our breasts with the brightness of Thy names.

BAHÁ'U'LLÁH

11.
An Apology is the Superglue of Life

We are human beings and in that respect, we are very prone to making great many mistakes. The only other human tendency that surfaces through our mistakes is to pin the blame on someone else. As Dwight D. Eisenhower once said, "The search for a scapegoat is the easiest of all hunting expeditions;" it is always the owning up that is the most difficult part of having erred.

I remember as a child, I had cheated in a language examination while in grade three and not being able to cope with the guilt, I ran to my mother telling her that I had in fact cheated in my examination and she sent me off to own up to my language teacher. As difficult as it was, my mother made certain that I did so and after that one lesson learnt in early childhood, I realized the importance of admitting your mistake and that ensures that the conscious is eased off the burden of culpability and remorse.

It might take a long while to condition ourselves to lead a life of admitting our mistakes as we make them because the most primary question is of realizing that we have in fact erred because most often we feel so sure of our actions that even though our inner self might be crying itself hoarse over a mistake that we could have committed, on the surface of our existence we remain in denial about it. It truly takes a wise mind to recognize when it is making a mistake and a charitable heart to concede to that mistake but once we set ourselves on that path in life, all obstacles will naturally give way to a more guilt-free life.

Measure your soul in its actions and see for yourself if you have aggrieved anyone, merely apologizing then would amount to meager lip service and the words meant to simply sound good fail to make any impact on a heart in anguish. As G.K. Chesterton explains it to perfection, "A stiff apology is a second insult... The injured party does not want to be compensated because he has been wronged; he wants to be healed because he has been hurt."

You may think that the person aggrieved is justly so and that he may not deserve your apology but that is not how nature, our biggest teacher is. The flowers in your garden do not choose to bloom depending on how well you appreciate their beauty but they display their most magnificent colors knowing that when the time is right you shall stop by and be thankful for their beauty. Similarly, do what you must, irrespective of whether the other person deserves it or not and leave the rest for nature to take its own course, because as Lynn Johnston puts it, "An apology is the superglue of life. It can repair just about anything."

Tip

A Chinese proverb says: "Tell me and I forget. Show me and I remember. Have me do it and I understand." Imbibe the same and watch how speedily you learn from your mistakes. Do not be afraid of experimenting but if you end up making a mistake, write it down and patiently analyze what made you make the mistake and what you learnt out of it. Chances are that after deep introspection, you will be better prepared the next time around.

And remember, it takes a strong mind to say sorry, the weak hearted will try and squirm out of it.

Prayer

"Bless those who persecute you; bless and do not curse.
Rejoice with those who rejoice; mourn with those who mourn.
Live in harmony with one another.

Do not be proud, but be willing to associate with people of low position.

Do not be conceited.

Do not repay anyone evil for evil.

Be careful to do what is right in the eyes of everybody.

If it is possible, as far as it depends on you, live at peace with everyone.

Do not take revenge, my friends, but leave room for God's wrath, for it is written: 'It is mine to avenge; I will repay,' says the Lord.

On the contrary: 'if your enemy is hungry, feed him; if

he is thirsty, give him something to drink. In doing this, you will heap burning coals on his head.'

Do not be overcome by evil, but overcome evil with good."

(ROMANS 12:14-21).

12.
Love Conquers All

William Shakespeare had truly said that — "Love is a smoke made with the fume of sighs. Being purged, a fire sparkling in lover's eyes. Being vexed, a sea nourished with lover's tears. What is else? A Madness most discreet, a choking gall and a preserving sweet."

Love is an all encompassing truth of life, it is the only emotion as pure as the waters that filter down from the mountains to touch every living, breathing part of the world, it is the only feeling as calming as the silvery moonlight, the only sensation as warm as the sunlight that filters through our window panes. As Karen Sunde said, "To love is to receive a glimpse of heaven." It is the only emotion that propels us to experience the goodness of all other emotions; it is a feeling of contentment, the only sentiment that makes us feel complete and in harmony with the universe at large.

Love is that interplay of light and shadow that leaves us fascinated and wanting more. Love comes to everyone, lighthearted and dainty, like a butterfly upon a rose and it is this fragility of the emotion that we must understand to live it completely. It is but love that compelled Meera to search her self in Krsna and it is only in loving where the power of the cosmos lies.

Love is like the rainbow in the sky, a joy to those who get to see it and yet it cannot be captured within the palms of the hand no matter how much you might try and possess it. Which is why the famous adage "set the one you love free, if he comes back he is yours, if he doesn't, he never was", the truth of love lies in setting it free and the moment we can teach our hearts to let go is the moment that our hearts will also let go of fear and we will learn to truly venerate the emotion of loving.

We have often seen people who go in for heart surgery to have pace makers attached to their hearts, we should try and emulate the same and instead have peace makers in our hearts that turns all things of discord within us into reasons for melody and tunes within us and then we can sit back and watch as our soul takes flight into a waltz of loving and selflessness that will eventually merge with the oneness of the complete universe. Bertrand Russell wrote, "To fear love is to fear life, and those who fear life are already three parts dead."

The wisdom of love is in giving and doing so altruistically and then we will find that the more we give, the more we will find. As Mother Teresa said, "I have found the paradox that if I love until it hurts, then there is no hurt but only more love".

Exercise

This is a simple exercise that will enable you to love more freely and give all of the love you have without diluting it with the waters of jealousy, suspicion, expectations or anger. Take out five minutes in your day and imagine that the day that you are living is the last day of your life. Then try and think of the people whom you have not professed your love to and yet you would not want to die without letting them know. Pick up your phone and call up the people who come to your mind or send them a mail telling them exactly what they mean to you and how much you love them.

Use the same parameter, as though it were your last day and think of all those people whom you take for granted, as you draw up your list, also make a record of the things that you could do for the people on this list that will make them feel happy and also convey to them how much you love them. After you have figured out what it is that you would like to do for each person, set yourself a time frame within which you will accomplish communicating your love to all these people.

Try and make this exercise a weekly or fortnightly

habit because it is very easy to make relationships, but to sustain them takes a lot of nurturing and tender affection.

Prayer

Dear Lord,
I bring before you those, whom I love,
Watch over them,
And keep them safe from all harm.
Amen.

Love comforteth,
Like sunshine after rain.

Love ever gives, forgives, outlives,
And ever stands with open hands,
And while it lives it gives.
For this is love's prerogative,
To give, and give, and give.

God bless all those that I love.
God bless all those that love me.
God bless all those that love those that I love
And all those that love those that love me.

FROM A 17 CENTURY
NEEDLEWORK SAMPLER

13.
Nurture your Experiences, they are the Source of all Wisdom

Wieland had once said, " however learned or eloquent, man knows nothing truly that he has not learned from experience." This one statement is the most valid truth of human life. What makes us different from any other living being on this planet is our experience, quite like fingerprints, no matter how similar; one's experience cannot match another's.

Holding on to our experiences is the art of living, many people tend to shun their experiences if foul and overlook the agreeable ones searching for better experiences, but a truly wise person will collect all his / her experiences and string them in a fine garland, unique to himself / herself and wear it around the crown of wisdom. As the French proverb goes "I know by my own pot how others boil."

There is very little in this world that we can give to ourselves and the insight that our experience parts us with is a gift for life, we should only know how to nurture such wisdom and not relegate it to the backburners of our lives because it is experience alone that teaches us how not to burn our hands in fire. James Boswell had said, "Men are wise in proportion, not to their experience, but to their capacity for experience."

The delicacy lies in internalizing our experiences within our hearts and minds, for we are taught the same curriculum whilst being educated in school, but it is in the school of life that we are given invaluable lessons, each matchless and distinct and it is this education that shows us the path to better living.

Andre Gide once said, "An experience teaches ably the good observer: but far from seeking a lesson in it, everyone looks for an argument in experience, and everyone interprets the conclusion his own way." That is the flipside of looking at experiences with a closed perspective, there are always lessons laid out for us to be learnt but sometimes we choose to overlook such messages because we do not consider our experiences worth much but the day we begin to understand that our growth as human beings depends on what we learn from our experiences is the day the veil shall be taken off from our ignorance.

Exercise

Call you best friend over on a day when you both have some time to spend together. Make a stopover at a museum and walk through it together, taking in the paintings but do not evaluate them verbally as you walk through, alternatively you can also take a walk in the park together, again, not talking while you walk.

After you are done, sit together at a café or elsewhere and then assess what you saw. Even though you visited the same place together, you will realize that you observed different things about the same painting or saw diverse aspects about the park while you walked through it. This exercise will help you appreciate better that even though things around you might be the same, perspectives are what make them different for each one of us, and that is the lesson to be learnt about experiences. They are what make us different from another person and through this method; this consciousness will dawn upon us better and we will learn to value our individual experiences more.

Prayer

I asked for strength that I might achieve;
He made me weak that I might obey.
I asked for health that I might do great things;
He gave me grace that I might do better things.
I asked for riches that I might be happy;
He gave me poverty that I might be wise.
I asked for power that I might have the praise of men;
He gave me weakness that I might feel a need of God.
I asked for all things that I might enjoy life;
He gave me life that I might enjoy all things.
I received nothing I had asked for;
He gave me all I hoped for.

ANONYMOUS

14.

Forgiveness is the Key to Mend What lies Broken

Very often in life, we find ourselves standing alone, surrounded by a sea of people and yet feeling the sharp intense pain of loneliness, of feeling let down by people around us, holding ourselves responsible for expecting anything out of people at all. But then, expectation is bound to occur if we have duly attached ourselves to another person. Breaking free of attachment in such situations probably feels like an easier thing to do than anything else but the seed of the solution lies in forgiveness.

Holding a grudge against someone or to hold someone responsible for our anguish is a way of imprisoning our own souls because feelings of anger and resentment are like thick clouds of gloomy gray smoke and once they begin to enclose the soul then they begin to feed off it, rendering our soul dark and unforgiving as well. The Adi Granth endorses the same when it says, "When there is forgiveness, there is God himself," as does the Qu'ran when it says, "If you overlook and forgive, then lo! God is forgiving, merciful."

The key lies in sincere forgiveness that comes from the heart. As easy as it is to say that, it is unfortunately just as difficult to execute. Forgiveness too can be superficial where we convey to the other that we have in fact forgiven them but in some corner of our hearts, there still exists a feeling of bitterness and resentment, in that case, try and truly from the bottom of your heart indulge in the act of forgiveness. It is exonerating someone that will ease the burden off our karma and we will know ourselves to be free and liberated once we have liberated other people of our hatred and aggravation and instead replaced it with benevolence and understanding.

To not forgive someone would mean to turn the perennial seas of the heart into dead water because to hold a grudge against someone, you will have to take out affection from your heart and replace it with an attitude of detestation. The choice always lies in your hand, to forgive and spread the message of love and affection around you or to become engulfed in the fumes of dislike and hatred. As Dag Hammarskjold said, "Forgiveness is the answer to the child's dream of a miracle by which what is broken is made whole again, what is soiled is again made clean."

Reflection

It is very often that people knowingly or unwittingly make us go through a period of grief and agony and we do not want anything to do with them anymore or to see them again. In such a situation, one should ideally sit in the lap of nature or even in a room, alone and should do the following visualization with your eyes closed:

When surrounded by a feeling of condemnation, simply visualize your heart to be a vast field of green grass and beautiful shrubs on which the most glorious of all flowers grow. In the center of the field is the most beautiful shrub that is being wilted under the weight of a creeper growing around it. Now picture yourself walking towards the center of the grassland and manually uprooting the creeper with your bare hands. The shrub signifies the person against whom you hold a grudge and the creeper is the feeling of abhorrence for that person, by uprooting the creeper, you have rid your heart of all negative emotions for that person.

Now, around the very shrub, plant the seeds of the most beautiful flowers, majestic in their colors and magnificent in their fragrance. Planting the seeds is symbolic of replacing hatred in your heart for that person with the goodness of compassion and forgiveness.

Once you have visualized the above, then think about the person who has done wrong unto you, take his / her name, smile within yourself and visualize telling him / her that you have forgiven him / her.

When you open your eyes, you will find that your heart has shed itself of all negative emotions and is free to love and embrace again.

Prayer

The Track of the Sun
Across the Sky
Leaves its shining message,
Illuminating,
Strengthening,
Warming,
Us who are here,
Showing us we are not alone,
We are yet ALIVE!
And this fire
Our fire
Shall not die!

Atoni

15.
The Blank Paper Syndrome

There is a particular phenomenon that I have noticed, living in a family that constitutes of writers in one respect or the other, something that I have coined the 'blank paper syndrome'. This syndrome is when we are at work, all ready to start typing at the keys of the computer or penning our work of the day on paper but when we get down to it, there is a vacuum in our minds. Words seem to have gotten stuck behind a make believe wall in the mind and nothing seems to flow from the hands on to the computer or paper. Words seem frozen and the mind seems incapacitated to do the most mechanical of all tasks.

That is when we should sit back in our chairs and try and assess if something is causing us inherent anxiety. Rose F. Kennedy had once said, "Neither comprehension nor learning can take place in an atmosphere of anxiety." Most often we are facing a conflicting situation in our life and we decide to push it at the backburner of our day to complete other tasks that we have chosen for ourselves. The brain might consciously try and aid us in fulfilling our set goals for the day, but the heart that is feeling a sense of quandary will never be at rest to allow the mind to finish its tasks in peace. But, as George Michael puts it, "You'll never find peace of mind until you listen to your heart."

The heart is not a switch to be turned off for later use. It is the seat of our emotions, meant to be the threshold of veneration in the temples of our soul. We must knowingly first deal with all matters of the heart, settle a troubled thought in our head, resolve whatever situation of dilemma that we find ourselves in, and once we have stable for ourselves must we continue to resume our office or household work and then words will no longer seem suspended in a vacuum, it will all become a case of amplified expression thereafter because as Adam Duritz says, "Get right to the heart of matters. It's the heart that matters more."

Tip

Whenever you are in a dilemma, leave everything that you are doing aside and take out time to go for a stroll in the park or sit by yourself and listen to some comforting music. While doing either one of the exercises, try and think about what is troubling your heart and mind. You need not necessarily come up with a cure but such introspection will enable you to come out of your chaos feeling better.

Follow this with treating yourself to a colossal amount of your best-loved cuisine with a friend or your partner or maybe even alone if it makes you feel better and this time, do not count calories or watch what you eat, if you indulge your stomach, it will warm your heart and give it the strength to deal with your quandary better.

Meditation On Lord Ganesha

Gajaananam bhootaganaadisevitam
Kapittha jamboophala saara bhakshitam;
Umaasutam shoka vinaasha kaaranam
Namaami vighneshwara paada pankajam.

I worship the lotus feet of Ganesha, the son of Uma, the destroyer of all sorrows, who is served by the host of gods and elementals, and who takes the essence of the kapittha-jarnbu fruit (fruit resembling the bilwa fruit).

Ganesha is the God of auspices, when worshipped at the beginning of any new work; he brings together all successes and fortuity for the worshipper.

16.
Float upon the Stream, Embrace Everyone on the Way

Very often in our life we meet people who make us feel extremely joyous, people whose presence seems to make our heart want to sing and all our troubles seem to disappear like the stars in daylight when those people are around us and then there are people who are just the opposite. People, whose presence makes us feel some sort of abstract constriction in the heart and we seem to wither away in their presence.

It is but natural for us to want to spend time with the former kind of people and to shirk away from people who make us feel uneasy but the mantra of life lies in embracing both kinds of people. There are people whose positive energy our souls feed off, we bask in the goodness of their nature but then there are people who similarly need to derive their positivity from us and to shy away from them means breaking the link of nature.

The truth is that whenever you are around a distressed person, you are absorbing his / her energy but that energy does not remain the same when it comes to you, instead that energy gets transformed into the same positive energy that you exude.

To remain aloof from people who might need you to share their anguish with would mean that you are not giving your soul a chance to empathize and sympathize. It is very convenient, especially in today's day and age to shut off other people's problems from our lives if they have nothing to do with us, but that is when we close the doors of hearts to the biggest religion in the world - humanity. It is important for our lives to be complete that we spread whatever joy we have in us to extend to other people.

Think of Mother Teresa, a woman who found the meaning of her life in helping people selflessly, one need not stop working towards their goals in life and dedicate it to serving others but to take out some time to help others, our friends colleagues and family, that is sufficient reason for our soul to transcend into higher realms of understanding.

Exercise

There are some days when you might return home from work or college, even having met friends when you feel bogged down and exhausted in spirit. One reason of that could be the fact that the human aura is like a magnet and it attracts both positive and negative vibrations from other people's aura and excessive negative energy in the aura can make one feel depressed and miserable.

In such a situation, prepare yourself a bath in which you add about half a fistful salt crystals. Let the salt dissolve in the bathwater and then bathe your body with this treated water. Salt is the most effective element found in nature that can cleanse the aura since its absorption capacity is the highest and thus it absorbs all the negative energy that the aura might be carrying within itself.

Post the bath, you will find yourself rejuvenated and raring to meet a brand new day. This bath is specially effective in the morning since it will enhance the vitality and vigor of a new day.

Prayer

By the power and the truth of this practice,
May all beings have happiness, and the causes of happiness.
May all be free from sorrow, and the causes of sorrow.
May all never be separated from the sacred happiness
Which is free of sorrow.
And may all live in equanimity,
Without too much attachment and too much aversion,
And live believing in the equality of all that lives.

May all beings be filled with joy and peace.
May all beings everywhere,
The strong and the weak,
The great and the small,
The mean and the powerful,
The short and the long,
The subtle and the gross:
May all beings everywhere,
Seen and unseen,
Dwelling far off or nearby,
Being or waiting to become:
May all be filled with lasting joy.

Let no one deceive another,
Let no one anywhere despise another,
Let no one out of anger or resentment
Wish suffering on anyone at all.
Just as a mother with her own life
Protects her child, her only child, from harm,
So within yourself let grow
A boundless love for all creatures.

Let your love flow outward through the universe,
To its height, its depth, its broad extent,
A limitless love, without hatred or enmity.
Then as you stand or walk,
Sit or lie down,
As long as you are awake,
Strive for this with a one-pointed mind;
Your life will bring heaven to earth.

A PRAYER FROM
SUTTA NIPATA

17.
Be Patient Towards all that is Unanswered Within

Very often in life, we find ourselves facing a predicament, two things beckon when we can have just one and that is when at such crossroads we find our souls stretched and frayed. We do not know what road to take for both the things that face us are things that we covet and they are both contradictory.

In such situations, we need to calm the mind first. If we compel ourselves to make a decision in haste then it would come as no surprise if we regret it later because our heart, soul and mind need to be in perfect harmony before we can choose fittingly what it is that we want. At such times, we might feel pressurized by circumstances and people to make a swift choice but it is also at times like these that we need to disregard the pressure and look inwards to find the answer. The answer might take long in coming, but self-realization is a powerful medium of ridding the mind of all doubt.

To quote Rainer Maria Rilke, "Be patient toward all that is unsolved in your heart and try to love the questions themselves like locked rooms and like books that are written in a very foreign tongue. Do not now seek the answers, which cannot be given you because you would not be able to live them. And the point is, to live everything. Live the questions now. Perhaps you will find them gradually, without noticing it, and live along some distant day into the answer."

All we need to do when in a quandary is think about what it is that we really want and if we get what we yearn for, will it add to the substance of our lives or is it a mere temporary fascination that we have which will become meaningless as we understand life better? The heart is our channel to the inner consciousness that does not lie and once we feel the answer to our predicament coming truly from the heart, then the confusion gives way to crystal clear comprehension and most often the choice that we thus make, never fails us.

"If by renouncing a lesser happiness one may realize a greater happiness, let the wise man renounce the lesser, having regard for the greater."

DHAMMAPADA

Meditation

This is actually a very simple meditation really. Sit in a quiet place where you can afford to listen to your inner self. Take a seated or lying position that you find most comfortable. Now focus on your breathing till it becomes harmonious and melodic. Inhale at a count of three, hold your breath for another count of three and yet again exhale at a count of three, holding the breath again for a similar count. Continue breathing in the same fashion and visualize walking up to a warm and comfortable room that is filled with your favorite flowers and the walls are adorned with colorful and cheerful paintings. As you walk around the room, observe the plentiful plants that add yet more cheer to the room.

As you walk around the room, visualize two chests of drawers, each symbolizing the two personas of your problem and each has a key to unlock it on its top shelf. Decide which of the two drawers you will access and open the one you wish to. As you do that, keep in mind that both the drawers are symbolic of the predicament in your mind. When you open the drawer that you have opted for, it will automatically lead you to know what it is that your inner mind has decided for you. As much as this should not be the ultimate deciding factor, this meditation truly helps in making up one's mind.

After you have come to terms with the drawer that you have opened, lie back and smile to yourself with your eyes closed and reiterate to yourself that your heart knows what is best for you. Count till thirty and then slowly open your eyes, at the same time smiling to yourself and you are sure to feel energized post this.

Prayer

Take, O Lord, and receive my entire liberty,

My memory, my understanding and my whole will.

All that I am and all that I possess You have given me.

I surrender it all to You to be disposed of according to Your will.

Give me only Your love and Your grace;

With these I will be rich enough,

And will desire nothing more.

JESUIT—SAINT IGNATIUS LOYOLA —16TH CENTURY

18.
Stay Awake

On some days we might lie awake on our bed wondering if what we have in our lives so far is all that life is truly made of? We set ourselves wondering if we have actually crossed all the milestones of life that there are and after where we are in the current moment it would only seem like encore after encore at every subsequent stage of life. But Charles de Lint gives hope when he says, "Without mysteries, life would be very dull indeed. What would be left to strive for if everything were known?"

That is when we should look out of our windows and watch as the sun's rays play a game of light and shadows with our windowpanes. As Jon Bon Jovi explains, "Miracles happen everyday, change your perception of what a miracle is and you'll see them all around you." The sun is the same that sets every evening, the night brings with it the same moon that spreads its silvery mist all around and yet, each sunrise and moonset brings with it, its own special something, something that cannot be named but something that dreams are made of. Storm Jameson once said, "The only way to live is to accept each minute as an unrepeatable miracle, which is exactly what it is: a miracle and unrepeatable."

Life is also never the same, we might feel that we have seen it all and done it all but you don't know when it might spring a grand surprise for you and your life might never be the same again. Life is a lot like walking down the beach; you never know when you might stumble upon the most exquisite sea- shell that the waves have laid in your way because you were meant to have it.

There is always a great possibility that while on the journey called life, we might stumble upon love and happiness like never before because time and destiny meant for us to have it at a particular stage of life.

The key is staying awake because the show goes on till as long as you want it to, the moment that your spirit dampens is when the curtains of life will fall but till then its all a miracle waiting to happen in your life everyday. And on the lighter side of life, Pablo Picasso said, "Everything is a miracle. It is a miracle that one does not dissolve in one's bath like a lump of sugar."

Exercise

Whenever you feel that life has nothing new to offer to you, do a very simple exercise. Take a piece of long cloth, satin if you like to feel sensual or even a handkerchief will do. Now take this piece of cloth and walk up to your garden or to a park when there are relatively lesser people.

Now, blindfold yourself so that you cannot see anything around you. Now take small steps and use the gift of touch to sense the things around you. Try and touch the blades of grass on the soil, try and touch the petals of the flowers in the garden, feel each part of the flower and you will find that nothing is what you have known it to be before. Every sensation around you will evoke a different emotion because you have blocked once sense to heighten another. Use your sense of smell to distinguish the flowers in the park or garden, since your eyes will not be able to perceive anything, you will come to rely on the sense of smell for it. This experience promises to be not only new but it will also open your eyes to the fact that the things around you are the same but there is a lot more to be discovered in them from what you already know of them. This exercise will not only help you broaden your perspective, it will also enable you to experience the vastness and depth of the world around you and the inexhaustible treasures that are a part of it.

Prayer

Through your blessing, grace, and guidance,

Through the power of the light that streams from you:

May all my negative karma, destructive emotions,

Obscurations and blockages be purified and removed,

May I know myself forgiven

For all the harm I may have thought and done,

May I accomplish this profound practice of phowa,

And die a good and peaceful death,

And through the triumph of my death,

May I be able to benefit all other beings, living or dead.

TIBETAN BUDDHIST PHOWA PRACTICE

19.
Truth Comes in Shades of Gray

Gray is perhaps the most innocuous color in the spectrum but that is the real color of life. One very attention-grabbing facet of life is that it is never all white or black, never all good or bad and yet when we are living it, we expect to meet extremities at all times. It is said that too much of a good thing can also be harmful and that holds true for all aspects of living.

Like Baltasar Gracian rightly said, "the orange squeezed completely dry will only give bitterness", whenever we try and make something perfect, it will never succeed because life is such. Everything that surrounds us and happens to us is a complete package, a lot like a watermelon; it will have the goodness of its nectar but also the obstacles of its many seeds and just like we cannot buy a watermelon bereft of its seeds, we cannot have the joys of life without equally accepting its grief as well.

Nothing that exists in this world is all good or all bad because there are stages to everything, sometimes sweet and at others savory. The secret lies in living both the black and the white of life along with its various hues of gray and that is how when it is time for us to go to our graves, we will do so with a smile on our faces. The color of truth as Andre Gide says, is gray and that is what we often fail to observe. The most relevant of all realities of life will never tally with our boundaries of black and white because what is truth for one could well be an absolute lie for another and it is thus that all of what is real will only be found when the black and white are merged together.

We are but half men and women, there is within us yet another person waiting to be fulfilled and that awakening can only arise when we can overcome the colorblindness of seeing the mere black and white of life. There are many more emotions to be explored, which can only happen when we make peace with the gray of our lives.

The moment we cease to visualize the gray of our lives, as an intruder upon its extremities is when we will be able to see the warp and weft of life with clarity that we might have never experienced before because our veracity lies in the coming together of the good and the bad. Let the colors of life blossom unto yourself and then watch as it bears fruit.

Exercise

You may or may not have a green thumb but this is a simple gardening exercise. Buy from the closest mart, seeds of an exotic flower that you fancy immensely and along with it, also buy yourself a gardening kit in case you have not ventured into your garden or potted plants before. Now take these seeds and plant them in the oldest and most beaten up can or tin that you can find. Nurture this plant with care as you bring up a child till it is in full bloom, spreading its splendor all around.

Once the flower is in its majestic best, observe the can in which you planted it, you will realize that in its bloom, the flower is making the rusted tin also look superior. That is the lesson to be learnt about learning to take the good with the bad, when life brings you a fair balance of both black and white, internalize all the good things and perceive all the misery reflected in the goodness of the lessons that your soul gets to learn from it and you will begin to appreciate the color gray better.

Prayer

Humbly we pray that this mind

May be steadfast in us,

And that through these our hands,

And the hands of others

To whom thou shalt give the same spirit,

Thou wilt vouchsafe to endow

The human family with new mercies.

FRANCIS BACON

20.
Seek Beyond the Self

The greatest fools are the ones who think themselves to be the wisest. In my practice as a chromotherapist, I have come across many people whose lives have gone awry simply because they were so sure of what they were doing was right that even when they did do a wrong deed or make an incorrect choice they were so blinded by their feeling of knowing it all that they could not observe where they were going wrong. Bertrand Russell echoes the same thought in his quote, "The whole problem with the world is that fools and fanatics are always so certain of themselves, but wiser people so full of doubts."

There is an enormous difference between self-esteem and overconfidence but to cross over from one to another is just only a step away. There should never be a time in our lives where our self-esteem is suffering for that is when we fail to recognize our own worth and sink so low in our own approbation that we begin to doubt everything that we do and say, and that is the beginning of a state of under confidence and subsequent everyday distress in whatever that we do. Overconfidence on the other hand is easy to acquire and just as complicated to get rid of and gifted as all our minds are, it is not arduous to stay away from the obsession of the self that overconfidence can bring with it.

There is a famous Aesop's fable about a frog and an ox where a little frog says to the bigger frog, "Oh Father, I have seen such a terrible monster! It was as big as a mountain, with horns on its head, and a long tail, and it had hoofs divided in two."

"Quiet, child, quiet," said the old Frog, "that was only Farmer White's Ox. It isn't so big either; he may be a little bit taller than I, but I could easily make myself quite as broad; just you see." So he blew himself out as hard as he could. "Was he as big as that?" asked he.

"Oh, much bigger than that," said the young Frog.

Again the old one blew himself out, and asked the young one if the Ox was as big as that.

"Much bigger, father, bigger than that too," was the reply.

So the Frog took a deep breath, and blew and blew and blew, and bloated and swelled and engorged. And then he said: "I'm sure the Ox is not as big as how I am right now." But at this moment he burst.

This fable indicates just how self-conceit may lead to self-destruction.

When one becomes a little too sure of him or herself, then everybody else around that person seems a bit of a fool to that person. Advice and counsel from anyone else seems impertinent to that person and he/she starts to obsess over themselves alone. That is a perilous situation for not only the person concerned but for all other people who come into contact with that person and thus at every stage of our lives we should try and constantly sift our attitude to tell if we are simply being confident about our beliefs and opinions or if we are becoming imposing with them. A story of a Zen master is very famous and is told the world over, this story is about a university professor who went to see Nan-in, a Zen master: to find out more about Zen. Their meeting had just begun and first the master asked the professor to join him for tea. As they sat for tea, Nan-in began to pour tea for the professor and continued to pour it even after the cup was brimming over with tea. The professor cried out at watching this and said, "but master...no more tea will go in!" Nan-in looked up at the professor and replied, "Just as this cup, you are full of your own opinions and beliefs. How can I show you Zen unless you first empty your cup?"

There is an art in living life in the best possible way and Lao-Tzu glorifies that when he says, "He is strong who conquers others: he who conquers himself is mighty."

Meditation

Whenever you feel as if you might be increasingly disregarding other people emotions or beliefs, then indulge in a simple meditation.

Sit in a quiet place, take a comfortable position and close your eyes. Now relive the last day of your life that went by, incident by incident, not forgetting to count even the most innocuous person whom you met. Now visualize any conversation you might have had with all the people whom you met and recollect what they had to say to you. Also call to mind what you had to say to them and try and summon if you were truly listening to them or if you were simply hearing what they were saying. Try and recollect if you had an open mind while you were being spoken to or if you were smug in the belief that what the other person was saying was inconsequential.

What is important in this meditation is that when you are sitting by yourself, nobody is watching you or reading your thoughts so it is imperative that you do not lie to yourself. As soon as you think clearly with reason, the truth about how you perceive people will dawn on you and then you will know which patterns of your mind and heart to set right.

Realization is half the battle won, once our inner selves know where we are going wrong, our souls come with an inherent guide to fix such things...the idea is to let the heart take over and all else falls into place.

Prayer

O angel of God, my holy guardian, given to me from heaven, enlighten me this day, and save me from all evil.

Instruct me in doing good deeds, and set me on the path of salvation. Amen.

O angel of Christ, holy guardian and protector of my soul and body, forgive me everything wherein I have offended you every day of my life, and protect me from all influence and temptation of the Evil One.

May I never again anger God by my sins. Pray for me to the Lord, that He may make me worthy of the grace of the All-Holy Trinity, and of the blessed Mother of God, and of all the saints.

Amen.

ORTHODOX CHRISTIAN PRAYER

21.

Once Connected Two Souls Can Never Part

It is seen in moments when love fades away between two people that what was once the esteemed altar of piousness is replaces by intense sullenness and animosity. I have seen many relationships fade out where the two people in question cannot even remain good friends or even acquaintances for they turn into each others most unforgiving foes. Joseph Roux once said, "As long as we love, we lend to the beloved object qualities of the mind and heart which we deprive him of when the day of misunderstanding arrives."

Love is the emotion that brings out the best in a person and when we turn the same love into an instrument of grieving others then we desecrate the sanctity of the emotion at large. People come together as a means to feel love and to spread the same love around them wherever they go and that is how it should always remain no matter how many people or situations come between those people, because when two people love each other no matter how short lived it might be, they make together, some intense memories that should not be consecrated to the bitter emotions of hating and detestation because as Karen Sunde puts it, "To love is to receive a glimpse of heaven" and we condemn ourselves to hell if we let love turn into ashes in the mouth.

We must realize that soul mates must not necessarily unite in body to confer completeness upon their togetherness. Two people who have loved each other ever should never try and script a relationship of hating upon each other when once they have loved, they come far above the reach of negativity because once together in some units of space and time, two people's inner lives can never run parallel thereafter. As Frederick Buechner says, "You can kiss your family and friends good-bye and put miles between you, but at the same time you carry them with you in your heart, your mind, your stomach, because you do not just live in a world but a world lives in you.."

> "...in hours of bliss we oft have met,
> They could not always last.
> And though the present I regret,
> I am grateful for the past."

WILLIAM CONGREVE

Tip

Whenever you are spending time with a loved one and you have a moment that is out of the ordinary, and that could be taking a bus ride through the country side together or your partner plucking a flower for you, ensure that you have a way of retaining that moment in your heart forever. You can do that by either writing down all about the special moment and how you felt or you could simply save a souvenir from the special moment, i.e., press the flower so that you can retain it forever or keep the ticket to the bus ride safely.

After collecting such keepsakes, you heart will never be lonely no matter how far a loved one might be from you.

Prayer

Remember me when I am gone away,

Gone into the silent land;

When you can no more hold me by the hand

Nor I half turn to go yet turning stay.

Remember me when no more day by day

You tell me of our future that you planned:

Only remember me; you understand

It will be late to counsel then or pray.

Yet if you should forget me for a while

After afterwards remember, do not grieve:

For if the darkness and corruption leave

A vestige of the thoughts that I once had,
Better by far you should forget and smile

Than that you should remember and be sad.

CHRISTINA ROSSETTI (1830-1895)

22.
The Ready Reckoner to Live

Life is like the starting points that one gets at the beginning of a game show, how far we go adding more points or losing out in negative marking is for us to chart out. Everyone is handed but one life if we choose to disregard the concepts of past life and reincarnations and in that case we get but one chance to make or break its fortunes. The key to living life is to simply live it well. As Socrates put it to perfection "what counts is not to live but to live right".

Here's a list of the ten best things to do to live life to the fullest now that you find yourselves stuck with it:

- Learn to love yourself
- Make friends wherever you go, keep touching people's heart no matter how adverse a situation.
- Live every moment of your life as your final celebration
- Make a memory with whatever you are doing, even if its boiling water.
- Smile as much as you can, it takes away nothing from you and instead it wins you many more smiles.
- Laugh out loud every now and then.
- Blot out all negative emotions that might stain your soul and tear it.
- Too many precautions in life will end up making you look like a signpost, go ahead and live life with gay abandon every now and then.
- Have faith in whatever you do and whatever happens to you.

- Make a stunning departure whenever its time to bid adieu, leave behind a treasury of laughter and smiles. Make every exit worth a standing ovation!

Exercise

The list mentioned of the ten things to do is a mere starting point, depending from person to person; it will have various added extras and subtractions. Make a list of your own, a list of the things that you feel are important for a person to live life to the fullest. That list should contain at least ten points but there is no limit to how long it should be, add as many things as you deem befitting the list.

Now make thirty copies of that list (one for each day of the month) and then at the end of each night, before you sleep, mark the things on your list that you have lived out in the course of the day. Think about the things that were mentioned in your list and those, which you have implemented in the day. Usually you will find that you live out five of the ten things mentioned in your list. The idea is that since you now have a ready reckoner of how to live life king / queen size that you try and live out at least eight if not all ten of those things mentioned in your list.

Remember, we get only one chance at life and to achieve the best results we must do all that it takes to make this lifetime memorable for ourselves and those around us before we arrive at its expiry date.

Prayer

Oh Great Spirit, whose voice I hear in the winds

And whose breath gives life to everyone,

Hear me.

I come to you as one of your many children;

I am weak, I am small and I need your wisdom and your strength.

Let me walk in beauty, and make my eyes ever

Behold the red and purple sunsets.

Make my hands respect the things you have made,

And make my ears sharp so I may hear your voice.

Make me wise, so that I may understand what you

Have taught my people and

The lessons you have hidden in each leaf

And each rock.

I ask for wisdom and strength,

Not to be superior to my brothers, but to be able

To fight my greatest enemy, myself.

Make me ever ready to come before you with

Clean hands and a straight eye,

So as life fades away as a fading sunset,

My spirit may come to you without shame.

OJIBWA PRAYER

23.
Walk Beyond Time

I have never worn a wrist watch all of my life and as a result on some days I even get late reaching a particular destination and most people would think that I do not know how to keep time. The truth is that there should be some days in our lives that should be written off to wrists without watches, if not always. Time is a mere tool for maintaining the rhythm and synchronicity of life but we tend to consider it the master plan of the universe when it is not so.

There is a sense of timelessness about our individual lives as it is about the entire universe at large. All the things of life that are truly precious are fluid and timeless, like love and affection; such emotions are not spellbound within the arms of time. It is not to say that we ought to completely disregard time but there should be moments in our lives that should be free from the bondages of units of time and space.

Time exists as a unit for us only till as we want it to, we willfully surrender ourselves to time for if we choose to break its shackles then the world will fall into a different motion which can be felt with every beat of the heart because our heart knows how to keep its own time and we don't need a watch to tell us so. Sri Sri Ravi Shankar explains that the world is called 'Vishv' in Hindi, which means one endless moment. He adds that life is but one endless unit of time but we fail to see that because of our inherent shortsightedness. He further elucidates that when we are traveling a certain stretch by car, we can only see a kilometer or two ahead of ourselves but the same stretch when seen from the aerial perspective of an aircraft falls into a much-extended line of vision. He urges us to view life in a comparable vein, it is but an endless field laid upon us, but because of our myopic capacity to see life, we fail to see it as such.

Some moments of our lives should be kept aside, free of time, for ourselves and for those who love us. Seek your peace in that twinkling of the eye which has escaped the pace of time, find yourself in the silences that your watch doesn't allow you and you will begin to see the world from a perspective that you have never envisaged before. As Og Mandino said, "A day merely survived is no cause for celebration. No more busy work. No more hiding from success. Leave time, leave space, to grow. Now, Now! Not tomorrow!"

Time is one long infinite moment from when the first sign of life appeared on the planet and ever since, has seen the birth of life and life turning into ashes. On some days we should gift ourselves eras in but one moment of timelessness and then we will find a touch of immortality bestowed upon us.

Tip

Bring out all your crayons and paints and make yourself a stylized placard that says, "I have only today to live." Add beads, colored thread, playing cards and all other assortments that you feel closely connected to, they could be things that you like or symbols of things that you would like to do if you only had one more day to live. Make this board a constant reminder and string it up in a prominent place in your room where it compels you to read it at least once in a day.

Such a constant reminder will ensure that you live each day as if it were your last day!

Prayer

God, give us grace to accept with serenity

The things that cannot be changed,

Courage to change the things

Which should be changed,

And the wisdom to distinguish

The one from the other.

Living one day at a time,

Enjoying one moment at a time,

Accepting hardship as a pathway to peace,

Taking, as Jesus did,

This sinful world as it is,

Not as I would have it,
Trusting that You will make all things right,

If I surrender to Your will,

So that I may be reasonably happy in this life,

And supremely happy with You forever in the next.

Amen.

THE SERENITY PRAYER
—REINHOLD NIEBUHR

24.
Raise the Dust of Change on the Road to Life

We as people are often scared of change, we habitually like our lives to be lead on well treaded paths which may offer no excitement but nevertheless are familiar territories. In situations like these, if we are faced with a change that is the law of nature, then we close ourselves into our shells and try to resist the revision of our lives or a particular circumstance.

Change is an inevitable reality, nothing in this world remains the same and moulds are meant to be broken. Just as the green leaf of a summer tree must turn to yellow in autumn, so must the human life be in a constant motion of change. As children we have all played musical chairs where we must change seating to a musical tune and that act of changing chairs itself determines who wins the game. It is actually the game imitating life and as in the game, it is at first difficult to adapt to change but once we begin to hear the rhythms that change plays out then it is a mere matter of attuning our frequencies to such music and all else falls into a perfect pattern.

Watch the passages that life lays down at your feet, do not try and retreat from that course, instead accept them as rites of passage, a path that must be crossed to reach a new destination. King Whitney Jr. said, "Change has a considerable psychological impact on the human mind. To the fearful it is threatening because it means that things may get worse. To the hopeful it is encouraging because things may get better. To the confident it is inspiring because the challenge exists to make things better." If we shun change, then we are in essence recoiling from evolution...entering a new phase of life is like shedding the garment of our yesterday and wearing a new beginning upon our souls. Life will always bring us upon unfamiliar ground, there will always be a new challenge but wisdom lies in understanding that, as rivers must meet the seas so must new beginnings be embraced for all paths will ultimately bring us to the path of moksha.

As we walk on the sandy beaches of life, we will meet many new experiences and form many new relationships, let each such experience be a stepping stone to finding our centers within ourselves, not hurdles that prevent us from hearing our inner voices. Life is a planned harmonious whole that is set in motion by the laws of nature and to question change would mean stopping the wheel of time from turning.

Life is what we make of it, do not be afraid of what it brings to your threshold, instead embrace its uncertainty, its abstraction, let its fragrant haze engulf you for what might look like mist from afar is where we will find our course wrapped in a dream, waiting to be unfolded with the hands of passion and reason.

Exercise

If you find yourself to be someone who is particularly uneasy with the thought of change, then internalize a simple exercise that will prepare you for most changes that life brings with it. Once every fortnight, try and rework the interiors of your room or house. Every fifteen days, either add new elements to your room or rearrange the room in such a way that nothing in it looks the same. While attempting the exercise, try and get as experimental as you can since not only will the exercise enable you to adapt to changes faster but it will also solve the dual purpose of making you initiate change in your life in other areas as also encouraging you to get experimental with everything that surrounds you.

Initially you may not like the idea of changing something that already looks perfect to your eyes, but compel yourself to make a change in the interior, no matter how small, but it should look evidently significant. Taking the first step to initiate any kind of change is the most difficult and once you can manage to achieve that, the subsequent steps will all come very easily to you.

Prayer

May the road rise up to meet you.

May the wind be always at your back.

May the sun shine warm upon your face;

The rains fall soft upon your fields and until we meet again,

May God hold you in the palm of His hand.

TRADITIONAL GAELIC BLESSING

25.
Everyone is a Healer

Many people think that being a healer is a difficult thing to achieve but in all earnest, the simplest thing that one can become in life is to become a healer. As Mother Teresa said, "There is a light in this world, a healing spirit more powerful than any darkness we may encounter. We sometime lose sight of this force when there is suffering and too much pain. Then suddenly, the spirit will emerge through the lives of ordinary people who hear a call and answer in extraordinary ways."

There is within us, the spirit of healing and for that we need to have no art, we need no cards or the art of meditation for the greatest healing force in this world is love. Once we have come to appreciate the interdependence of all living and non-living beings in nature, we will find ourselves connected to everything around us, attached with the force of imperceptible energy which resembles a colossal fishing net and all beings are sheltered under that net. Just as how tugging one end of a blanket rearranges the entire blanket, similarly sending out a bit of love by one person from within the net can reorder the entire cosmos. Herman Melville says, "We cannot live only for ourselves. A thousand fibers connect us with our fellow men."

To give out love to this world, we first need to rid ourselves of the weight of hatred upon our souls. We have to first learn to live together, to share, to realize that there is nobody walking this planet who is a stranger to us, everyone is everyone's brethren and that it is only by giving that our hearts will receive more. As the Bhagawad Gita says, "He who hates no single being, is friendly and compassionate, free from self-regard and vanity, the same in good and evil, patient: contended, ever devout, subdued in soul, firm in purpose, fixed on Me in heart and mind and who worships Me, is dear to Me." The spirit that lives within you is the same that lives within each one of us, in every plant and animal as well and when we begin to understand the underlying unity that holds us all together, we will no longer know hate or jealousy. When we fail to see the familiar thread that ties us together is when we draw boundaries and make walls. Instead we must learn to make bridges and all the beauty of the world will open up to us.

The Dhammapada states, "To avoid all evil, to cultivate good and to cleanse one's mind- this is the teaching of the Buddha. Enduring patience is the highest austerity. One is not a true monk who harms another, nor a real renunciate who oppresses others." Hate is a mere bondage, it engulfs you and ties you to its intense darkness, it is the virus that multiplies by thousands if your heart bears its seed and love is the only antidote to hatred. Love needs no reason for it to grow; it needs no season to nurture it either. Once we have cleared our mind of the remnants of negativity then we have tended its soil for the seeds of love to be planted.

Find all the kindness in your heart and pour it

forth towards the world, then you will find that there are many thirsty seekers, who with one drop of your love will be satiated. One touch of the hand, one upward curve of the lips can touch many hearts and make many links as well. This world needs the link of your love to make the chain stronger and this love is rendered the healing potion for life.

A healer is merely one who can heal with one touch of love and this simple virtue that all of us possess makes us all healers certified by God. All we need is to seize the rainbows within us and spread its glory amongst all others, beyond the man made bondages of age, creed and caste. We do not need guns; we need instead flowers in our baskets and a song in our hearts, so start humming from today!

Tip

Whenever you have some spare time at hand, make out a list stating reasons why you love the following:

- Your partner
- Your family
- Friends
- Relatives
- People at work
- Acquaintances
- People in your neighborhood
- Your countrymen
- The world at large

Think of all the reasons you possibly can till your list keeps growing bigger and bigger, involve all of your friends and relatives in the same exercise and keep adding more and more reasons. You might not know it, but you will be starting a journey of peace that is created within one person but will soon engulf all those around you and in your own little but significant way, you will be giving peace a chance.

Prayer

OM MANI PADME HUM
Buddhist seed mantra

Thus the six syllables, OM MANI PADME HUM, mean that in dependence on the practice of a path that is an indivisible union of method and wisdom, one can transform one's impure body, speech and mind into the pure exalted body, speech and mind of a Buddha. It is said that one should not seek for the spirit of Buddhism outside of oneself; the substances for the achievement of Buddhism are within.

As Maitreya says in his Sublime Continuum of the Great Vehicle (Uttaratantra), all beings naturally have the Buddha nature in their own continuum. We have within us the seed of purity, the essence of a One Gone thus (Tathagatabarbha) that is to be transformed and fully developed into the spirit of Buddhism.

26.

The Right Recipe for the Perfect Speech

This is the era of sugar free; the sweetest of desserts

can be bought off the shelves of stores that proudly announce everything to be sugar free and with fewer calories than before. There is one zone though that should never be sugar-free and that is our speech. As Samuel Coleridge once said, "Language is the armory of the human mind, and at once contains the trophies of its past and the weapons of its future conquests."

Our hearts might hold the most noble of intentions for other people but our speech might convey just the opposite. Acid is meant to clean drains not to be a content of our speech. Most people use profanities because they feel agitated or they might say spiteful things because we all know that the word is mightier than the sword but the same word should be used as if coated with honey and filled with the goodness of love not as a replacement to a physical assault on someone.

Saying kind words and words of encouragement does not take away anything from us, instead it fills our hearts with joy and happiness as well. We might not think much of paying someone a compliment or appreciating someone's hard work but when such words of thoughtfulness fall upon the listener's ears, it brightens up their entire day. On the other hand if we choose to make the frown on our foreheads our best friend and discourteous words their accomplice then we can turn the most loving of friends into crude adversaries.

The choice always lies in our hands and it is for us to make the most of what God has gifted us with, the best advice is to leave the sugar-free for aspartame tablets and to take the sweeter route to life through our own speech.

Exercise

This is a simple exercise that will enable you to understand the effectiveness of the sweetness of speech and also help you make it a part of everyday life. Pick a colleague at work or an acquaintance in the neighborhood or in college whom you know, but not too well and have never spoken to for very long. Now, intentionally walk up to person that you have identified and tell them something about themselves that you really appreciate; it could be the way they write a presentation or the kind of clothes that they wear.

Only, ensure that you mean whatever you are telling the person and say whatever that you have to tell them in the sweetest way possible. Make a compliment sound like one and then watch as the expression on their faces change, no matter what their demeanor so far, they will surely have a smile on their face and that is the power of a word well spoken, it can turn the unhappiest of people into people full of joy and fervor.

Once you see for yourself, the strength that lies in the sweetness of speech, you will automatically begin to imbibe it in your everyday life and then you will become a source of joy for many people around you.

Prayer

May the wind blow sweetness,
The rivers flow sweetness,
The herbs grow sweetness,
For the People of Truth!

Sweet be the night,
Sweet the dawn,
Sweet be earth's fragrance,
Sweet be our Heaven!

May the tree afford us sweetness,
The sunshine sweetness,
Our cows yield sweetness —
Milk in plenty!

SOURCE: THE RIG VEGA

27.
Make Big Plans and Deliver!!

Another very significant lesson for daily use in our lives is that we must always finish whatever it is that we start. Our imagination is an immensely potent tool, it is something that fires our system with its probabilities and prospects and it is this very commanding instrument that sets us out to achieve newer and bigger things for ourselves. While we embark on an unsullied journey we also raise with it other people's expectations and that slowly turns the journey into one with a fair amount of baggage. Daniel Hudson Burnham once said, "Make no little plans; they have no magic to stir men's blood and probably themselves will not be realized. Make big plans; aim high in hope and work, remembering that a noble, logical diagram once recorded will not die, but long after we are gone be a living thing, asserting itself with ever-growing insistence."

But it also very often happens that while on our way to achieve our goals, we lose enthusiasm and hope for it half way through and decide to give up on whatever it is that we have decided to take up. That is not only defeatist behavior but also a surefire way of never getting into the habit of fighting a battle and seeing it till its very end. Patience is like a rare orchid, it takes time to nurture it but once grown, it can be very rewarding. A patient man fears nothing, he / she knows that with perseverance everything finds a way out and to draw upon this very facet can help a person achieve his / her goals in life without having to hold their heads mid-way and wonder why they took upon the task in any case.

On the way to achieve what we want to, there might be inexhaustible obstacles but to let them deter us would mean giving up without trying the extent of our valor. Each attempt to achieve anything in life is like standing in the heart of a battlefield and to take flight from the field would mean that our inner self is incapacitated. Arnold Bennett had once said, "Having once decided to achieve a certain task, achieve it at all costs of tedium and distaste. The gain in self-confidence of having accomplished a tiresome labor is immense." It does hold true that whatever is worth achieving in life will surely, without fail, come with a measure of obstacles and the exigency of being resolute and the way to achieve the goals lies in being perseverant because as a Chinese proverb goes, with time and patience alone does a mulberry leaf become a silk gown.

Brian Adams once quoted, "Learn the art of patience. Apply discipline to your thoughts when they become anxious over the outcome of a goal. Impatience breeds anxiety, fear, discouragement and failure. Patience creates confidence, decisiveness, and a rational outlook, which eventually leads to success."

Baptize your weaknesses with the strength of courage and resolve for our limitations are but golden chains that our brain ties us to, the key lies in understanding that the brain might feel insufficiently equipped to deal with a situation but if we let our minds take over then nothing can stop us from accomplishing the ideals that we set for ourselves.

Exercise

Every morning when you awaken from slumber, allow yourself five extra minutes in bed and use this time to do a simple meditation. Close your eyes while smiling to yourself, thank your God and Mother Nature for gifting your life with so much beauty around it and then proceed to visualize the tasks in your itinerary for the day.

Visualize working through every task that you have set for yourself for the day and then observe as you finish the assignment. Feel the happiness within yourself of having finished the work in time and to perfection, you will find that your soul is already brimming over with elation in the anticipation of the feeling of satisfaction that comes from finishing a task in time.

This positive deliberation will compel you during the day to achieve the feeling of gratification that you had felt in the beginning of the day at the thought of finishing your work and you will find yourself not only finishing the work that you have undertaken but also giving it the best that you have.

Once you learn to internalize this feeling then nothing will be able to stop you from achieving success in whatever that you set out to do.

Prayer

Yatha tvam kripaya bhutya
Tejasa mahimaujasa
Jushta isa gunaih sarvais
Tato 'si bhagavan prabhuhu

"O my Lord, because You are endowed with causeless mercy, all opulence, all prowess and all glories, strength and transcendental qualities, You are the Supreme Personality of Godhead, the master of everyone." (Bhag. 6.19.5)

Invocation to Lord Vishnu, the preserver of all life on earth.

28.
*H*earing the *S*ounds of *S*ilence

And then there are days of broken wings, when you will lie back on wet grass and wonder...

Life is never about one unbreakable string of fragility; it's about what we choose to make of it. Reality is not what the eyes perceive, it is what the heart knows and it is not to say that the heart cannot be in doubt, but the heart finds its own reason only that we should know how to hear the silences of the heart. Ausonius had once said, "He who does not know how to be silent will not know how to speak" and so silence is as important to our being as is speech, as we are growing up, in our formative years, we are taught the importance of speech and its correct usage as well, but what most people forget to educate us about is the substance that lies in silences. Mahatma Gandhi, a man most revered in India said about silences that "In the attitude of silence the soul finds the path in a clearer light, and what is elusive and deceptive resolves itself into crystal clearness."

Life is a long journey and the only map to it is our heart, once we know how to read its directions, the destination becomes clearer and the passage even more extraordinary. Looking up a directory unfortunately cannot unearth such maps, they lie embedded deep within us and it takes but the tool of silence to understand the text of the map.

Silences within us possess more strength than words could ever contain but to hear the silences we have to shut out the meaningless noises that surround us always. Emptiness of the within is not always reason for loneliness, sometimes the very emptiness gives us the room to pour in worthy emotions and feelings, for you can only add more when there is the space to, and if our minds and hearts are always cluttered then where would we find within them the shelves to place our higher emotions?

As much as we need to be with other people most of the times, we also need our silences just as much. When we walk through a forest we will observe the same that the multitude of trees make up one endless forest but no tree stands close enough to another to overpower or eclipse it and that is how the human life should be, close enough to hold each others hand but distant enough that one's inner voices can be heard. Lynn Johnston had said, "The most profound statements are often said in silence" and once we internalize the truth behind the statement we will begin to adapt to our silences which will only enable us to grow as human beings.

It is indeed finding this very balance that will help us find our roots within, the roots that connect us to the fiber of the universe and finding such ground will win us both our share of the earth and the heavens. For our heart knows the secrets of the universe but our ears will only hear it in the silences, which we bestow upon it.

Reflection

Take some time out in a day whenever you are most at peace and free from interruptions. The time could vary from five minutes to five hours but what is imperative is that you be with yourself. Try and find yourself the most comfortable chair or mattress that you can and seat yourself in the position that you find most relaxing. Ensure that you are warm if it is winter and your body is cool enough if it is summer. Close your eyes and identify all the noises that you can hear around you, after doing so, visualize all these noises fading away gradually till you cannot hear them anymore.

After the noises in the environment have faded away from your hearing frequencies, then try and focus on your heartbeat, try and feel its thrust inside you and hear its beat within yourself. Once you have attuned yourself to be able to hear your heart, then smile upon yourself, within yourself and try and watch as your deepest thoughts reveal themselves to you since you have accustomed your senses to minimize all other worldly reverberations and clatter that surround you and are prepared to hear what your inner self has to tell you.

You will be astonished at the thoughts that come to you when you are introspecting in your silences, there will dawn moments of revelations that will not only help you understand your inner-self better but they will also help you to organize your relationships and emotions better.

Once you get attuned to hearing your silences, soon you will require no meditational stance for it; you will be able to hear your inner self amongst thousands of people and you will never find yourself lonely again.

Prayer

Dear Lord and Father of mankind,

Forgive our foolish ways!
Reclothe us in our rightful mind;
In purer lives your service find,
In deeper reverence, praise.
Drop your still dews of quietness
Till all our strivings cease:
Take from our lives the strain and stress,
And let our ordered lives confess
The beauty of your peace.

JOHN GREENLEAF WHITTIER
(1807-1892)

29.
Dream Big and Aim for the Moon

Dreaming is not an exercise limited to when we are asleep. Dreaming is something that we must indulge in always. Our eyes should always carry a dream in them, as should our hearts. The logic behind dreaming is simple actually, energy follows thoughts and that is the ultimate truth. If we have a dream within us and we think of making that dream turn into reality, then in essence we are creating positive vibrations around the wish that we want fulfilled and such optimistic thoughts can help one achieve anything, even moksha.

Many a times we dream big and then stop ourselves from doing so almost immediately because we feel incapable of making it come true but once we allow ourselves the freedom to dream big, then all the smaller dreams in the foray will start coming true first. Its is only when we dream of attaining the moon that we will first end up with a fistful of stars if nothing else, but if we only aim for the stars then we will end up with dust in our palms alone.

To be able to savor a fruit in the peak of its season, one first needs to plant the seed of the fruit and dreaming is like planting the seed of one's achievement, as soon as there is a dream in the consciousness, the cosmos will find pathways that lead to the fulfillment of the dream. As we walk the journeys of life, we should go on scattering the seeds of our dreams, there is no telling which one might take shape first but eventually all dreams do come true.

Dreams are boundless, the only limit to a dream is your own imagination, so craft your dreams with the wings of goodness and the purity of heart and watch as your dreams take flight. Garth Brooks and Victoria Shaw wrote in their song 'The River':

"You know a dream is like a river, ever changing as it flows.

And a dreamer's just a vessel that must follow where it goes.

Trying to learn from what's behind you and never knowing what's in store

makes each day a constant battle just to stay between the shores.

And I will sail my vessel 'til the river runs dry.

Like a bird upon the wind, these waters are my sky.

I'll never reach my destination if I never try,

So I will sail my vessel 'til the river runs dry.

Too many times we stand aside and let the water slip away.

To what we put off 'til tomorrow has now become today.

So don't you sit upon the shore and say you're satisfied.

Choose to chance the rapids and dare to dance the tides."

Exercise

Dreaming is an inherent activity that once if we set our minds to do then the rest falls into place with perfect precision but the question is how do we get ourselves to begin to dream in the first place. The answer is quite simple really. Make a visit to your local market and try and single out a dream catcher that you take a fancy to, otherwise make your own dream catcher at home using feathers, wool, beads and whatever other material that you like. The only thing to consider is that it should be a piece of art that pulls at the strings of your heart and is something that you find visually very appealing. Traditionally dream catchers are hung above a person's bed and are said to trap all the nightmares that a person might have and only filters down the beautiful dreams to the person, above whose head the dream catcher hangs.

Take the dream catcher and place it exactly above your bed, not only will it make all your nightmares disappear but it will also become a constant hanging reminder of the fact that dreaming is the first step to success and when you see its symbol hanging in your room everyday, your mind will subliminally keep reiterating the same message again and again and it will be a matter of time before you not only begin to dream big but also see those dreams coming true for yourself.

Prayer

Dear Lord, I may not see the sun and moon lose their light. I may not witness rivers turn red,

Or stars fall from the sky.

Yet there are times when my world becomes unhinged and the foundations of what I believe crack and dissolve.

Give me the grace to believe that Your power is at working the turmoil of my life.

Lead me to remember that Your power is greater than all evil, and though the world may rock and sometimes break, it will in time be transformed by Your Love.

ANONYMOUS

30.

Celebrate Life as if it Were Your Last Day

I was traveling to my office one day when I saw someone's car that proclaimed from its bumper sticker 'A day without sunshine is, like night.' Suddenly it dawned upon me that life is in fact too short to spend it counting the places where it hurts. We have only one lifetime to fit into it all that we can, and then to add to the sense of urgency is also the fact that this one moment is all that we recognize beyond doubt without a thought to the future. As Oprah Winfrey quoted in the September 2002 issue of the O magazine, "Breathe. Let go. And remind yourself that this very moment is the only one you know you have for sure." The fact that each moment of our life is both extraordinary and unique to us makes it reason enough to celebrate it at every step, at every passage.

We do not need a reason, a birth or a marriage or a festival to celebrate because in essence celebration happens from within, when the heart learns to find the silver lining to the darkest of all clouds, it involuntarily begins to float in the skies of merriment, much like how the peacock by design shall dance in the rain and it is a law of nature, this law also applies to our spirits, we only sometimes tend to ignore it. Amanda Bradley had once said, "Celebrate the happiness that friends are always giving, make every day a holiday and celebrate just living!" Nature is constantly giving us a reason to celebrate; there are always marvelous fireworks around us, we just have to stop to smell the flowers because they are always there, fragrant for all of us but only those make time for it can smell it.

The simplest way of finding a reason to celebrate life is to find the humor in our lives. Tracing life's lighter side can give us a perspective of life really being quite like a carnival with its ups and downs, a mere roller coaster ride. Osho too meant the same when he said, "I say unto you that suffering is not holding you, you are holding suffering...and when you become good at the art of letting go, then you'll come to realize what you were dragging around with you. And for that, no one else other than you was responsible...the truth is that existence wants festival...because when you are unhappy, you also throw unhappiness all around."

If you look around you, you will find a thousand reasons to laugh and be joyous about it is all about what the eyes want to see, if you want your spirit to soar then merely petting a furry animal will make your life feel vindicated but if you choose to be sad and gloomy then even the sight of sparkles in the sky or a comet whizzing through the sky will seem infuriating to you. As Barbara Hoffman says, "Stop worrying about the potholes in the road and celebrate the journey!"

Do not simply survive your days and exist while you could really be living. Today is all that you have and today is in your hands to make it into a holiday or to drag it around on its feet. To quote Oprah Winfrey again, "The more you praise and celebrate your life, the more there is in life to celebrate."

Tip

It doesn't take much to celebrate life, just keep trying to find more and more reasons to be happy and it will come to you naturally. On the other hand if there is day when you are feeling exceptionally exhilarated, then throw a small party for all your like-minded friends where you completely indulge yourself with the ornamentation of the party venue, pull out all your candles, get all the streamers and balloons that you can find and while you are at it, get part caps for all the invitees, age irrespective.

Top it with an enormously scrumptious cake enveloped with multi hued candles. Tweak out all your old games and turn your venue into a mini playroom. Have music playing constantly in the background and ensure that everybody gets to shake a leg at least once.

Have fun and celebrate life how it ought to be celebrated.

Prayer

I celebrate myself, and sing myself,
And what I assume you shall assume,
For every atom belonging to me as good belongs to you.

I loaf and invite my soul,
I lean and loaf at my ease observing a spear of summer grass.

My tongue, every atom of my blood, form'd from this soil, this air,
Born here of parents born here from parents the same, and their parents the same,

I, now thirty-seven years old in perfect health begin,
Hoping to cease not till death.

Creeds and schools in abeyance,
Retiring back a while sufficed at what they are, but never forgotten,
I harbor for good or bad, I permit to speak at every hazard,
Nature without check with original energy.

Verse 1 - song of myself
WALT WHITMAN

Prayer for healing

I realize that the body is not separate from the mind.

As I let go my old attitude toward my body I appreciate the influence of the spirit and soul

And I embrace my body and my entire self.

My body is a reflection of my thoughts.

As I give myself positive affirmations I release my negative emotions and thoughts

And I let my body be healed as well as my mind

I am forgetting that I am not my disease

And that I can stop the disease to please

I am not my mistakes and my failures

And I am not my past and my pains

I am awakening from my illusions

I fear and I choose not to

I suffer and I choose not to

I am sick and I choose not to

I am willing to get better and heal

I am lifted above the areas of my pain

I am rising beyond my suffering

I am releasing my desperation

I understand and accept my insecurities

I feel compassion toward my pains

I surrender my terror for it is not real

I surrender my fear as I surrender all things

I open my heart, my soul and my body

I know the strength and the power of faith

*I feel the process of cleansing and
I welcome the miracle of healing*

May every cell of my body be healthy

May every feeling of my soul be radiant

May every thought of my being be vibrant

May every action be aligned with love

I accept my imperfections as

I release my fears and doubts

I invite a healing light as

I become illumined and light

I trust the process and the journey

I receive peace and calmness

I learn from my mistakes and I also learn from happiness

I want to rise up joyful and strong

I will be born anew into health

And into happiness, peace and love
I am aware of the need to forgive

I am grateful for the opportunity to grow

I am confident that I will succeed

I am expecting my freedom and healing

I listen well to my body

I follow my intuition

I find all the knowledge and I apply all the insights

I search for the lessons within

I release all shame and blaming

I let go of all false thinking

I let myself be free and happy

I cast out all the impurities from my body, heart and soul

I do my best to fill myself with love

I expect a miracle with relaxed anticipation

I am my own best doctor and advisor
I am a catalyst for healing

I am a producer of health

I am a creator of happiness

Thank you for my healing body

Thank you for my gentle soul

Thank you for my strong spirit

Thank you for the chance to heal

I am willing to be enlightened as I am blessed with this wisdom

I deserve to be healthy and happy and I claim my perfect health again

I am ONE and I am LOVING.

I am HERE and I am NOW.

I am HEALED and I am WHOLE.

Thank YOU. Let it Be! And SO IT IS!

PRAYER FOR HEALING
—DARINA STOYANOVA

Epilogue

Hope is one of the most evocative element of optimism and this book puts together the dynamism of encouraging words and quotes, the power of meditation and the healing intensity of prayer to guide the reader through thirty days of the month with inspiration, motivation and a zeal for life.

This book is meant to act, as an easy- to- understand tool of daily meditation, which can be imbibed effortlessly to enhance daily living and to celebrate every day of your life with renewed vigor.